SINGIN' IN THE RAIN

THE MGM LIBRARY OF FILM SCRIPTS

Ninotchka

North by Northwest

Adam's Rib

Singin' in the Rain

A Day at the Races

A Night at the Opera

Singin' in the Rain

Story and screenplay by Betty Comden and Adolph Green
with an introduction by the authors

A VIKING FILM BOOK

NEW YORK / *The Viking Press*

72-14483

CREDITS *(see film still 1)*

Production	Metro-Goldwyn-Mayer
Produced by	Arthur Freed
Directed by	Gene Kelly and Stanley Donen
Written by	Betty Comden and Adolph Green
Musical Director	Lennie Hayton
Orchestrations by	Conrad Salinger, Wally Heglin, and Skip Martin

Songs:

"Would You?", "Singin' in the Rain," "All I Do Is Dream of You," "I've Got a Feeling You're Fooling," "Wedding of the Painted Doll," "Should I?", "Make 'Em Laugh," "You Were Meant for Me," "You Are My Lucky Star," "Fit as a Fiddle and Ready for Love," "Good Mornin' " by — Arthur Freed (lyrics); Nacio Herb Brown (music)

"Moses" by	Betty Comden, Adolph Green, and Roger Edens
Vocal arrangements by	Jeff Alexander
Director of Photography	Harold Rosson
Art Directors	Cedric Gibbons and Randall Duell
Set decorations by	Edwin B. Willis and Jacques Mapes
Special effects by	Warren Newcombe and Irving G. Ries, A.S.C.
Film Editor	Adrienne Fazan

v

Color Consultants	Henri Jaffa, James Gooch
Recording Supervisor	Douglas Shearer
Hair styles	Sydney Guilaroff
Makeup	William Tuttle
Length	9,228 ft.
Time	103 minutes
Released in	1952

C A S T

DON LOCKWOOD	Gene Kelly
COSMO BROWN	Donald O'Connor
KATHY SELDEN	Debbie Reynolds
LINA LAMONT	Jean Hagen
R. F. SIMPSON	Millard Mitchell
ZELDA ZANDERS	Rita Moreno
ROSCOE DEXTER	Douglas Fowley
DANCER	Cyd Charisse
DORA BAILEY	Madge Blake
ROD	King Donovan
PHOEBE DINSMORE, DICTION COACH	Kathleen Freeman
DICTION COACH	Bobby Watson
SID PHILLIPS, ASSISTANT DIRECTOR	Tommy Farrell
MALE LEAD IN "BEAUTIFUL GIRL" NUMBER	Jimmie Thompson
ASSISTANT DIRECTOR	Dan Foster
WARDROBE WOMAN	Margaret Bert
HAIRDRESSER	Mae Clark
OLGA MARA	Judy Landon
BARON DE LA BOUVET DE LA TOULON	John Dodsworth

vi

J. C. SPENDRILL III	Stuart Holmes
DON AS A BOY	Dennis Ross
VILLAIN IN WESTERN, BERT	Bill Lewin
PHIL, COWBOY HERO	Richard Emory
MAN ON SCREEN	Julius Tannen
LADIES IN WAITING	Dawn Addams, Elaine Stewart
VILLAIN, "DUELING CAVALIER" AND "BROADWAY RHYTHM"	Carl Milletaire
ORCHESTRA LEADER	Jac George
VALLEE IMPERSONATOR	Wilson Wood
AUDIENCE	Dorothy Patrick, William Lester, Charles Evans, Joi Lansing
FENCERS	Dave Sharpe, Russ Saunders

Russ Saunders doubles for Gene Kelly.

NOTE: Except for a few minor alterations, and the *post facto* descriptions of the musical numbers and montages created by director–choreographers Kelly and Donen, the other differences between the script of *Singin' in the Rain* and the film itself are covered in the Introduction. In this version we are presenting an account of what is in the film itself prepared by the authors of the script, Betty Comden and Adolph Green.

SINGIN' IN THE RAIN

All we knew about our assignment when we arrived in Hollywood in late May 1950 was that we were to write an original story and screenplay, as well as the lyrics, for a new musical picture. We had rushed out there in answer to an urgent "there's-not-a-moment-to-lose" crisis command from MGM, only to find every studio shut down and the whole place deserted. It looked very much the way Hollywood does right now on an average business day. Actually, all that had happened then was that everyone had taken off for a six-day Decoration Day weekend, leaving us to grind our teeth to the eyeballs in frustration, and run up six days of epic phone bills calling our loved ones back East.

At the time we were pioneers in bicoastal living, continuing to write for the theater in New York, our home, and coming out West periodically, to do a movie, and then return. By then we had written several pictures, the latest of which was the adaptation of our own first Broadway show, *On the Town*. The film had enjoyed financial and critical success, and the public had happily accepted the concept of an intimate movie musical in which almost all the musical numbers were handled by a small group of principals in realistic situations, some of them actually photographed on location in the streets of New York. It was also the first directorial assignment for Gene Kelly and Stanley Donen.

We always worked in what was known as the "Freed Unit." This was presided over by producer Arthur Freed from his three-room office suite in the imposing Thalberg or Administration Building, affectionately called "the Iron Lung." Our office was a simple monastic cell down the hall, which, because of our transiency, we never tried to make even remotely livable. The Freed Unit was something quite special in Hollywood, with conditions that permitted us to function somewhat the way we would in doing a show in New York. The writer was not treated as part of an assembly line in the old Hollywood tradition, which placed him at the bottom of the social structure, with the ego-crushing certainty that forty other scriptwriters would obliterate any trace of his work before it reached the screen.* Arthur also had a gift for importing, or taking chances on, people of the theater, allowing them to develop into moviemakers with a free-swinging spirit—Vincente Minnelli, Gene Kelly, Stanley Donen, Alan Jay Lerner, Oliver Smith, Michael Kidd, and the two of us. Down through the years and up until today, Arthur Freed has always referred to us as "the kids," sometimes warmly, as in "Hiya, kids" or "I'd like you to meet 'the kids,' " or sometimes impatiently (at a story conference), as in "For Chrissakes, kids, no one will believe that!" Assisting in all departments, as musical supervisor, sometimes script shepherd, arranger, associate producer, general coordinator of production— sometimes one or all of these—was Roger Edens, invaluable and devoted to Freed, and whose lapels we often clutched, and drenched with tears in moments of despair. In the late forties and early fifties the musicals emerging from this group, conducted and orchestrated mainly by Lennie Hayton and Conrad Salinger, had a kind of style and taste, filmic verve and inventiveness, that gave them the individual stamp of the Freed Unit, and a number of them survive, not as "camp" or sociological curiosa, but as films to be enjoyed, admired, and even wondered at—expressions of a form that has all but vanished.

When everyone returned from their interminable holiday that June in 1950, we were summoned, unslept and nervous, to a meeting in Arthur's office, where we were finally to discover why

---

* Writers were considered "the authors" unless disastrously proved otherwise, and were usually included in discussions of all aspects of production.

we had been rushed out there. Sun-drenched and relaxed after his rest, and surrounded by orchids from his vast greenhouses, Arthur greeted us warmly, inquired after families and friends, quoted the grosses of *South Pacific* from *Variety*, read us letters from Gian-Carlo Menotti and Irving Berlin, and after some further discussion of the state of the theater in New York, and phone calls to his brother Hugo at the orchid ranch, and to Oscar Levant on Stage 27, he said, "C'mon, kids, let's have some lunch." Arthur was trying not to tell us something. Somewhere around four that afternoon, after some prodding from us, he let it be known with a proud but shy chuckle that we had been assigned to write an original story and screenplay using songs from the extensive catalogue of lyricist Arthur Freed (the same) and composer Nacio Herb Brown (how many people can there be named "Nacio Herb Brown"?). Whatever came out of our creative hoppers, or out of two hopping mad creators, was to be called *Singin' in the Rain*. We gulped a gulp that could be heard around the world, and then followed a long silence during which the orchids around us seemed to grow into the man-eating variety. Finally we said, "But, Arthur, what about our new contract? It says, with all names spelled out, that Comden and Green are to write the lyrics unless the score is by (1) Irving Berlin, (2) Cole Porter, (3) Rodgers and Hammerstein." Arthur said, "Kids, I never heard of any such clause. Now, about *Singin' in the Rain*——" Bolstered by our knowledge of that magical clause, we sneered imperiously, skulked out of the office, and went on strike. After two war-torn weeks, during which we repeatedly accused Arthur of reneging on an official document, some flutter of the gut told us to read our contract. With the help of our new agent, Irving Lazar, using his bifocals as the Geiger counter to unearth the magical phrase, we learned there was no such thing. It was the emperor's new clause, a total fabrication of our former agent. "Kids," said Irving, "*anyone* can write lyrics for your picture—Berlin, Porter, R. and H., Freed, Karloff, Lugosi,

Johnny Weissmuller—you name it. My suggestion is you write 'Singin' in the Rain' at the top of a page, followed by 'Fade-in,' and don't stop until you come to 'That's all, folks.' "

So we began working on *Singin' in the Rain* like rats trapped in a burning barn. And let it be known for the record that Freed was very sweet and tolerant with us rats—didn't chase us with a broom or anything.

Later that very day we met with Roger around his piano in the Freed office and surveyed the sprawling stacks of Freed-Brown songs in sheet-music form, ranging all the way from "Should I?" to "Would You?" The late sun was just hitting the sign outside "Smith and Salisbury, Mortuary" next door, and we felt like walking over and lying down. We riffled through the songs as Roger played and sang them in his Southern colonel's whiskey baritone, and several possible stories suggested themselves. For instance, "The Wedding of the Painted Doll" could well have been the basis for a story about a painted doll who got married.

But as Roger kept playing, and we hummed along, we began in spite of ourselves to get excited. Many of them were famous songs, standards, bristling with vitality and part of the nation's collective unconscious—"Broadway Melody," "Broadway Rhythm," "You Are My Lucky Star," "Fit as a Fiddle," "You Were Meant for Me," and the title song itself, an irresistible ode to optimism which no one can possibly sing without acting out the line "There's a smile on my face." We knew one thing about the story. There would have to be some scene where there would be rain, and the leading man (Howard Keel? Van Johnson? Fred Astaire? Gene Kelly?) would be singin' in it. Many of these songs had been written by Freed and Brown for the earliest musical pictures made, between 1929 and 1931, during the painful transition from silence to sound, and it occurred to us that, rather than try to use them in a sophisticated, contemporary story, or a gay-nineties extravaganza, they would bloom at their happiest in something that took place in the very period in which they had been

4

written. With this decision made we began to feel the ground beneath our feet at last. We both knew the period intimately and were amateur authorities on silent films and early talkies, long before Cinema 1 and 2 was a subject taught in every kindergarten in the country.

The studio grapevine reached us that Howard Keel had been penciled in for the lead, and we made a few dispirited stabs at a yarn about a minor Western actor in silents who makes it big with the advent of sound as a singing cowboy. But our thoughts kept coming back to the dramatic upheavals of that period, when great careers were wrecked because the public's image of a favorite would be instantly destroyed by a voice that did not match the fabled face. We remembered particularly the downfall of John Gilbert, the reigning king of the silent screen in 1928, whose career was finished off by one talking picture, in which, with his director's encouragement, he improvised his own love scene, consisting of the phrase "I love you" repeated many times with growing intensity, exactly as he had done it the year before in front of the silent camera. The audience screamed with laughter. We decided our leading character should be just such a star. The trick, of course, was to make the stuff of tragedy like this fit into a lighthearted satirical comedy that featured fifteen or twenty Freed-Brown songs along the way. Our silent star would have to survive his downfall and make good as a musical star, and to give *that* story point a faint air of credibility, we had better establish our hero as someone who had had a song-and-dance vaudeville background before he entered pictures. Such a character felt more to us like Gene Kelly than Howard Keel.

Gene was one of our oldest friends from New York, as was Stanley Donen. We had first met Gene when we were in a revue at the Westport Country Playhouse one summer, he hoofing it up alone, and the two of us performing as part of a satirical act called "The Revuers." Later, when we had reached the dizzy heights of the Rainbow Room, Gene, still an unknown, was sud-

5

denly announced by the M.C. there as doing a tryout appearance for one show. Not long after, our paths crossed again, when he, the newly acclaimed Broadway star of *Pal Joey*, came down to the Village Vanguard to see his old pals, the Revuers, who had followed their heady climb to the sixty-fifth floor of the RCA Building by plummeting swiftly back down to the Vanguard cellar where they had started. Later, in Hollywood, a big movie star, Gene was to feed us often, and watch us perform tirelessly in his living room, writing having replaced performing in our careers, but not in our hearts and throats. Stanley was there, too, having started as a dancer in *Pal Joey*, and coming out to Hollywood when Gene did, to work as his assistant, and then co-director.

After their outstanding success as the directing team of *On the Town*, what we none too secretly hoped for was to reunite the four of us, with Gene again as star. But Gene was now, deservedly, at that happy moment when everyone wanted him for everything, and had he expressed the desire to film Kafka's "Metamorphosis" featuring the "Million-Legged Cockroach Ballet," the studio would have considered it a smart commercial move, and gone all the way with him. It was impossible for us to approach him, because he was deeply involved, head and feet, starring in and choreographing *An American in Paris*, which was shooting on the lot under Vincente Minnelli's direction. We kept seeing him all the time socially, but he let us know, in a friendly way, he was going to pick his next venture very carefully, and would rather not know what we were up to, so he could judge the finished script impartially.

In the meantime we spent an agonizing month trying to get a grip on ourselves and our screenplay. We finally had what seemed to be three possible opening sequences of a picture: a big silent-movie premiere in New York; a magazine interview with the star in Hollywood telling a phony life story; a sequence from the silent movie being premiered in New York, the star meeting the girl in New York, losing her, and going back to Hollywood. After staring for hours at a time at this seemingly insoluble mess, in which the story never seemed to get started, we would wander down to the set where *An American in Paris* was shooting, and feel even more wretched in the face of this assured, inevitably successful reality, rolling along with its thundering playbacks, swinging cranes, and jubilant actors, and its little Paris street, so achingly authentic that Arthur Freed could sit in the sidewalk café and quip to no one in particular, "I can sit here and feel homesick for Hollywood."

Our depression deepened as our story refused to move, and our feeling that we were involved in something ghoulish rather than comic was reinforced by the atmosphere of the place we were living in. It was a miniature *Sunset Boulevard* house, once owned by silent star Marie Prevost, which we had taken with mixed laughter and shudders because the price was right. The place screamed, in its tattered elegance, of high times in the twenties, with its glory suddenly extinguished. There was no body floating in the swimming pool, but tons of soggy leaves filled the deeper-than-wide concrete oblong, gloomily hidden from the sun at all times of the day; torn strips of faded awning flapped mournfully against the terrace windows; and inside the living room, furnished mainly with peeling gilt and needlepoint pieces and an urn containing God knows whose ashes, was the crowning touch—an inlaid concert grand player piano, its piano roll stuck from there to eternity somewhere in the middle of "Fascinatin' Rhythm." It was in this very room, one late afternoon, that we decided to kick the nightmarish grip of doom that had settled over us, and do something realistic: we would give MGM back the money they had paid us thus far, tell them we had failed, and go home.

A couple of hours later we were jumping up and down with glee, like Gene, Donald, and Debbie in the "Good Mornin'" song and dance in the movie *Singin' in the Rain* itself. My (Betty's) husband, Steve, had just arrived from New York and, knowing us rather well, was not too surprised to find us slumped in our familiar Dostoyevskian attitudes. At some point we grabbed him and read him our goulash of openings, to illustrate the hopelessness of the situation. Much to our amazement, Steve, a reticent chuckler, was roaring throughout, and asked, offhandedly, why, instead of abandoning the project, didn't we use *all* the openings? This led to the Eureka moment of realizing that maybe it could work if the action never went to New York, but all took place in Hollywood: the premiere, the interview in front of the theater before the stars go in, the shots of the silent movie itself, the backstage scene, the star's escape from his fans and his meeting the girl on Hollywood Boulevard, instead of Fifth Avenue. It seems pitifully obvious now, bordering on the moronic, but at the time we felt like Champollion deciphering the Rosetta Stone. From here on, the gates were open and the writing of the screenplay gushed in a relatively exuberant flow. We tapped the roots of our memories and experiences without editing ourselves when our ideas got wild, satirical, and extravagantly nonsensical. To our gratified surprise, not only did Roger seem delighted with it all, but Arthur, to whom we read each section as we completed it, gave it his happy approval.*

At Arthur's suggestion, Gene, who was by now finished shooting *An American in Paris*, was given a script to read, and we geared ourselves for a friendly refusal. Instead, he and Stanley Donen, who had also read it, came rushing over to us in the commissary the next day bursting with enthusiasm and filled with ideas which they imparted to us over our usual lunch of L. B. Mayer matzo-ball soup and surrealist song parodies. We started meeting with them instantly for final changes and rewrites, going over the script shot by shot. In addition to their outstanding skill in integrating all the elements of a musical film, our old friendship with them, and their knowledge of our work from our early performing days, made it easy for them to use many ideas and visual details that might have seemed irrelevant or a total mystery to anyone else.

The success of the film and its continued life over the years has much to do with our four-way mental radar, Gene and Stanley's

* The final go-ahead had to come from Dore Schary, who had recently replaced L. B. Mayer as head of the studio.

brilliant execution, and their sure professionalism while maintaining an air of effortless, carefree spontaneity. Also, one of the two directors gave a great performance. Just as we knew from the start, there was a scene where there was rain, and the leading man was singin' in it. What we hadn't written into the script was "Here Gene Kelly does perhaps the outstanding solo number of his career." Today, ironically enough, this exuberant, joyous expression of love of life is achieving a new kind of identity through Stanley Kubrick's *A Clockwork Orange*, where it is so devastatingly and chillingly used as an a cappella song and dance of mindless violence.

We went back to New York, leaving behind a lyric composed of tongue twisters starting with "Moses supposes his toes-es are roses," which Roger Edens put to music, making it the one non-Freed-Brown contribution to the score. We also learned, as the shooting date approached, that "The Wedding of the Painted Doll," which we had painfully wedged into the script as a cheering-up number for Donald O'Connor, had been replaced by a new song by Arthur and Mr. Brown, "Make 'Em Laugh." For this number Gene and Stanley took every piece of zany gymnastic clowning and surrealist vaudeville bit Donald had saved up in his body, and worked them into an insane classic unlike any other before or since.

Some months later, while out-of-town in Philadelphia going through the life-and-death throes of a revue we were involved with, we got a call from Gene and Stanley which seemed by that time to be coming from another galaxy. We had written a protracted love scene with a song-and-dance medley for Gene and Debbie Reynolds that involved touring many different sets all over the studio lot, but our directors wanted to change all that to a romantic love scene inside an empty sound stage where Gene would sing one song only, and do a romantic dance with Debbie. Could we run it up and mail it right out, please? We wrenched our minds away from the great Bert Lahr just two blocks away at the Shubert

Theatre despondently being hilarious in the ninety-five degree July Philadelphia heat, and time-machined ourselves back into *Singin' in the Rain* long enough to fill the order. It worked. So did the picture.

A few years ago we were in Paris with my (Betty's) husband, Steve, and my (Adolph's) wife, Phyllis, at a party, and were rendered breathless and awe-struck by the news that François Truffaut was right across the room from us. Suddenly a small, lithe figure came sliding across at us like a hockey player zooming over the ice. It was Truffaut himself, and he was breathless and awe-struck at meeting the authors of *Chantons sous la pluie*. In total disbelief we heard him go on to say, through his interpreter, that he had seen the film many many times, knew every frame of it, felt it was a classic, and that he and Alain Resnais, among others, went to see it regularly at a little theater called the Pagode, where it was even at that moment in the middle of a several-month run. This is a scene we never could have dreamed of that day at MGM when we went on strike because we did not want to write anything to be called *Singin' in the Rain*.

Nor could we have known that *Time* magazine would refer to it as one of the great "watershed" pictures (we have been assured it's not because of its title), or that Pauline Kael would one day write of it, "This exuberant and malicious satire of Hollywood in the late twenties is perhaps the most enjoyable of all movie musicals—just about the best Hollywood musical of all time," or that it would make the "Ten Best" lists of a number of publications all over the world, that it is constantly being studied in schools and revived, or that it would ever be published, as here and now it is, in glorious black and white.

—BETTY COMDEN and ADOLPH GREEN

Grauman's Chinese Theater—Hollywood

The scene is Hollywood in 1927, at the peak of the silent-movie era just prior to the introduction of sound pictures. It is the night of a big premiere. First we see huge beams of light searching the sky from big searchlights placed around the theater. We see the front of the Chinese Theater and enormous crowds along Hollywood Boulevard, and from the clothes of the people, we see that we are in the late 1920's. The marquee reads: PREMIERE TONIGHT—BIGGEST PICTURE OF 1927—DON LOCKWOOD AND LINA LAMONT IN "THE ROYAL RASCAL."

A couple of kids have climbed a palm tree and are looking at the sign. The police are holding back surging crowds which are pressing against ropes forming an aisle from the street to the entrance to the theater. The aisle is covered with red carpeting. A girl is clutching a fan magazine (Screen Digest—25¢) on the cover of which we see a picture of two movie stars and the heading "Lockwood and Lamont—Reel Life or Re-al Life Romance?" About three-quarters of the way up the aisle to the theater is a large, old-fashioned microphone, and to either side high poles topped with the flaring horns of an early public-address system. At the microphone stands Dora Bailey, a smartly dressed, matronly woman, a leading film columnist, who is addressing the crowd. She bears an unmistakable resemblance in both looks and voice to Louella Parsons.

DORA *(highly excited; in an overecstatic, gushy voice)*: This is Dora Bailey, ladies and gentlemen—talking to you from the front of the Chinese Theater in Hollywood. What a night, ladies and gentlemen—what a night! Every star in Hollywood's heaven is

11

here to make Monumental Pictures' premiere of *The Royal Rascal* the outstanding event of 1927. Everyone is breathlessly awaiting the arrival of Lina Lamont and Don Lockwood. Oh—

A shriek goes up from the crowd as a limousine pulls up in front of the theater.

DORA *(continuing)*: Look who's arriving now. It's that famous "Zip Girl" of the screen, the darling of the flapper set, Zelda Zanders—

Zelda Zanders, a flaming "It Girl" type, shimmies up the aisle accompanied by a very old doddering man in evening clothes.

—and her new red-hot pash—J. Cumberland Spendrill III, that well-known eligible bachelor.

CROWD *(rising and screaming)*: Ohhhhhhhhhh!

A MAN IN THE CROWD *(besides himself)*: Zelda! Ohhhh! Zelda!

Zelda poses with Spendrill III as photographers cluster around and light bulbs flash. They turn and go into the theater.

DORA: Zelda's had so much unhappiness. I hope this time it's really love.

Another limousine has pulled up and an exaggeratedly exotic woman of the Jetta Goudal–Nita Naldi variety steps out, wrapped in a long black cape. She is accompanied by a suave, be-moustached type in top hat and tails.

DORA: And look who's just arrived. It's that exotic star Olga Mara and her new husband, the Baron de la Bouvet de la Toulon.

CROWD: Ohhhhhhhh!

As Olga and the Baron proceed grandly up to the theater, she lets the cape open, and drags it slinkily along the ground, while photographers' bulbs flash.

DORA: They've been married two months already, but still as happy as newlyweds.

Another car has pulled up.

DORA: Well, well, well, it's—

There is an expectant hush. Then a man gets out of the car, starts up the aisle, dressed in evening clothes, boyish and anonymous-looking. It is Cosmo Brown. The crowd that has begun to lean forward expectantly is puzzled and disappointed.

CROWD *(sighing)*: Ohhhhh!

DORA *(continuing)*: Cosmo Brown.

Cosmo looks around, smiling embarrassedly, then stops next to Dora as she goes on.

Cosmo is Don Lockwood's best friend. He plays the piano on the set for Don and Lina to get them into those romantic moods.

Suddenly she is terribly excited.

Oh, oh, folks, this is it! This is it!

Two motorcycle policemen come roaring past the front of the theater and stop, followed by a super-limousine that does likewise. A liveried doorman steps forward to open the door as the crowd cheers in expectation, and photographers rush forward to capture the great moment.

DORA *(transported)*: *(See film stills 2, 3, 4.)* The stars of tonight's picture, those romantic lovers of the screen—Don Lockwood and Lina Lamont!

Policemen are pushing photographers back, and as the blur of bodies clears away, we see Don Lockwood and Lina Lamont standing in front of the limousine door. They are a truly dazzling sight, and the crowd goes insane, welling and surging against the ropes. Don is a dashingly handsome, buoyantly athletic-looking young man. Over his evening suit he is wearing a white camel-hair coat with a fold-over belt with matching soft-brimmed white hat, and is sporting a million-watt white-toothed smile. Lina is the epitome of classic patrician beauty, regal, elegant, and slightly aloof, a vision of devastating loveliness. They are both waving at the crowd, and Don throws kisses in their direction, to a response of deafening cheers. The screaming crowd is held back. One woman faints against the arms of two policemen. Lina and Don walk forward, still

13

waving, and step up to greet Dora, with Cosmo still standing beside her, and they all cluster around the microphone. Don shakes hands with Cosmo.

DORA: Ladies and gentlemen, when you look at this gorgeous couple, it's no wonder they're a household name all over the world, like bacon and eggs—Lockwood and Lamont!

From now on we see that Don does all the public-appearance talking for the two of them, while Lina just smiles, with a certain false graciousness, covering her annoyance.

DORA *(gushing)*: Don, you can tell me confidentially, are these rumors true that wedding bells are soon to ring for you and Lina?

DON: Well, Lina and I have no statement to make at the present time. We're just good friends.

DORA: You've come a long way together, Don. Won't you tell us how it all happened?

DON: Well, Lina and I have made a number of pictures together.

DORA: Oh, no, no, Don. I want your story from the beginning.

DON *(looking around self-effacingly)*: Oh, Dora, not in front of all these people.

CROWD *(as one)*: Yes!

DORA: But, Don, the story of your success is an inspiration to young people all over the world. Please!

This interview is to be considered as a number, during which, in ironic contrast to Don's voice giving a fabricated biography, we see what really took place in Don's life and career.

DON: Well, to begin with, any story of my career would have to include my lifelong friend, Cosmo Brown. We were kids together—grew up together—worked together—

DORA: Yes?

DON *(with hammy, false humility)*: Well, Dora—I've had one motto which I've always lived by—Dignity—always Dignity. This was instilled in me by Mum and Dad from the very beginning. They sent me to the best schools—including dancing school. That's where

14

I first met—Cosmo. And with him I used to perform for all Mum and Dad's society friends.

A Disreputable-looking Poolroom
Don, as a small boy in ragged clothes, is tap-dancing as tough poolroom characters throw him an occasional penny. Cosmo as a small boy is playing the harmonica.
DON'S VOICE: They used to make such a fuss over me.
A burly-looking saloon keeper grabs the boys as they bend to pick up the coins and carries them through the swinging doors.
DON'S VOICE: Then if I was very good, I was allowed to accompany Mum and Dad to the theater. They brought me up on Shaw, Molière, the finest of the classics—

The Front of an Old Nickelodeon Theater
There is a poster of a girl in African safari outfit in the clutches of a gorilla; the poster reads: "The Dangers of Drucilla—with Esme Gray—12th Episode." We see the boys sneak past the ticket taker and go in.

In Front of the Chinese Theater
DON: To this we added rigorous musical training—at the Conservatory of Fine Arts.

A Dingy Café
Don and Cosmo, now grown up, still in ragged clothes, are playing respectively a fiddle and a piano—in a band. (See film still 5.)
DON'S VOICE: We then rounded out our apprenticeship in the arts at the most exclusive dramatics academy.
A sign saying AMATEUR NIGHT.

15

The Stage of an Extremely Tawdry Burlesque House

We get a brief flash of Don and Cosmo performing a violent low-comic act of the "Three Stooges" type. Don and Cosmo get the hook which sweeps them offstage while they fall and protest. (See film still 6.)

DON'S VOICE: At all times, Dora, the motto remained—Dignity— always Dignity. In a few years, Cosmo and I were ready to embark on a dance-concert tour. We played the finest symphonic halls in the country—

Brief montage of whistle stops: DEAD MAN'S FANG, ARIZONA; OAT MEAL, NEBRASKA; COYOTEVILLE, NEW MEXICO.

Over all of them we see Don playing violin and Cosmo piano.

Stage of a Cheap Vaudeville Theater

Don and Cosmo perform "Fit as a Fiddle." Cosmo picks up a violin, and he and Don do a song-dance and violin routine, vigorous and wild, ending up walking forward on their knees. (See film still 7.)

DON'S VOICE: Audiences everywhere—adored us.

The audience is booing—several holding their noses.

DON'S VOICE: Finally, we decided to come to sunny California. . . .

In Front of an Employment Office

It is raining. HELP WANTED *signs are in view. Don and Cosmo are standing under the awning, their collars turned up, looking drenched and forlorn.*

DON'S VOICE: We were stranded here—we were *staying* here resting up when the offers from the movie studios started pouring in. Finally, we sorted them out and decided to favor Monumental Pictures—

A studio gate—Monumental Pictures. We see people going

16

in—and go through onto the lot. Inside the studio, Don is at the piano, Cosmo on violin playing mood music on the set of a typical Western bar as seen in cowboy pictures. We see a scene of violence. The villain, a dirty be-moustached fellow, is clutching the beautiful Lina Lamont in his arms. She is in dance-hall costume of the frontier period and is struggling to get free. We see the director and cameraman shooting the scene.

DIRECTOR (ROSCOE DEXTER, *dressed in riding boots and breeches and visored cap and shouting through a megaphone*): Okay, Lina— you don't like him! You hate him! You're resisting him! Keep that mood music going!

The actors follow the directions he gives.

DEXTER: Okay, now, Phil—you come in!

A cowboy-hero type comes dashing through the swinging doors. He registers the scene.

DEXTER: Keep on grinding! Now you see her, Phil!

Bert pushes Phil back and punches him.

DEXTER: That's it! Now, here's the bit, Bert, where you get it in the stomach!

Phil gives him a terrific punch in the stomach. Bert backs up and crashes his back against the edge of the bar. He crumbles to the floor.

DEXTER: Cut! No, no, that wasn't right, Bert! You're supposed to go head over heels over the bar and crash into the glasses. Try it again. Okay, Bert! Bert!

There is no answer.

DEXTER (*with some annoyance*): That's swell, just swell! Take him away, fellas.

Two men carry Bert off.

DEXTER: You'll be all right, Bert. We've lost more darn stunt men on this picture. Take us hours to get a new one over from Central Casting! (*He looks harassed*)

DON (*putting down his violin and going over to him*): Oh, Mr. Dexter, I think I can do that for you.

DEXTER: What, you? You're a musician.

COSMO (dryly): That's a moot point.

DEXTER (reconsidering): No kidding! What's your name?

DON (with satirical eagerness): Don Lockwood, sir, but the fellas all call me Donald.

DEXTER: Wise guy, huh? All right, I'll try you. Get this guy into Bert's suit, and remember, Lockwood, you may be trading that fiddle in for a harp.

Don has rapidly changed into cowboy shirt and hat.

DEXTER: Okay, Phil, come in. Now, you see her. Now, here's where you get it right on the jaw!

They do the scene over again. Don, punched by Phil, does a terrific back somersault over the bar, crashes into the glasses, and disappears behind the bar.

DEXTER: Ah! That was wonderful!

Don looks at Lina, who looks away disdainfully.

DON (dusting himself off casually): Got any other little chores you want done in this picture?

DEXTER: Plenty.

Don and Dexter shake hands.

Series of shots: Airfield; Don in the cockpit of an old biplane, waves, lowers goggles over his eyes.

DON (waving): Okay!

Don in airplane moving along the ground. It crashes into a house which is left in splinters.

Countryside: Don on a motorcycle—he looks and waves— lowers goggles down over his eyes.

Don, driving the motorcycle to the edge of a cliff and over into water 150 feet below.

Don, in Civil War uniform, looks and waves, runs toward a burning shack and into it. It explodes.

DON'S VOICE: My roles in these films were urbane, sophisticated— suave—

Outside Lina's Tent

Lina is resting against a board in front of her tent. A woman finishes doing her nails and exits. Don enters and goes over to her.

DON *(eagerly)*: Hello, Miss Lamont.

Lina barely glances up at him, annoyed at being addressed by such a lowly creature.

DON: I'm Don Lockwood, the stunt man. It's been a real pleasure working with you.

Lina looks up contemptuously and turns her back, ignoring his outstretched hand. Don looks at it embarrassedly. Dexter comes running up to him.

DEXTER: Hey, Don!

With Dexter we see R. F. Simpson, an authoritative, commanding figure.

DEXTER: Don, I want you to meet the producer of the picture, Mr. R. F. Simpson.

DON: Hello.

SIMPSON *(heartily)*: How do you do, son. I just saw some of the rushes for the picture and asked Dexter here who the team of stunt men were, and he said it was all you. I think you've got something, Don. I'm going to put you and Lina together in a picture. Come over to my office after lunch. We'll discuss a contract.

DON *(excited and impressed)*: Thanks, Mr. Simpson. *(See film still 8.)*

All through this, Lina has been all ears, and now turns to Don with a big smile. Simpson and Dexter exit. Don, who has noticed the big switch in Lina's attitude, now leans toward her insinuatingly.

DON *(in a husky, sexy tone)*: Well, Miss Lamont, doing anything tonight?

Lina looks up at him with a big seductive smile and shakes her head, putting her arm through his.

19

DON (*removing her arm*): That's funny—I'm busy.

He walks away, leaving her open-mouthed and furious. She kicks him.

DON'S VOICE: Well, Lina and I have had the same wonderful relationship ever since.

In Front of Grauman's

DON (*into the microphone*): But most important of all, I continue living up to my motto. Dignity—always Dignity.

DORA: Thank you, Don. And I'm sure you and Lina will continue making movie history tonight in your greatest picture, *The Royal Rascal*.

They all go into the theater as the crowd roars and the photographers snap pictures.

Inside Grauman's Chinese Theater

We see the audience looking toward the screen, where we see a small image of the film playing.

Here we see a black-and-white silent movie with titles. We see Don and Lina in Three Musketeers *period costumes kissing in a castle garden in front of a hedge.*

TITLE: Tonight the world is ours. Tonight we are alone.

They kiss. Don and Lina break from the kiss. He puts his hand behind his ear, listening suspiciously.

TITLE (*Don*): I think I hear a footstep.

We see a man come toward them, sword drawn. Don duels with him—hurls him over the stairway. We see Lina in the doorway, arms outstretched, and mouthing his name.

TITLE: Philippe!

Don reacts, rushes back to her, and they embrace.

In the audience, two girls are watching.

GIRL (*sighing*): She's so refined. I think I'll kill myself.

On screen, Don, in a series of fantastic gymnastics and heroics of a Fairbanks nature, fights off and kills a horde of attackers.

As he kills the last, we see Lina standing on the balcony, arms outstretched, and mouthing his name.

TITLE: Philippe!

Lina comes down the stairway as Don goes to her. They embrace and kiss, and a superimposed title reads: THE END.

The lights come up, and there is wild applause. The audience stands up and starts yelling for the stars.

On the stage of the theater a red-plush curtain has closed over the screen. From the wings enter Don and Lina, to applause. Lina opens her mouth as if to speak, and Don cuts in.

DON: Thank you, ladies and gentlemen—

Lina tries again.

DON (*gracious, but still cutting her off*): We are pretty darned thrilled at your response to *The Royal Rascal.* It was fun making it, and I hope you had fun seeing it tonight.

There is applause.

Lina tries again.

DON: We screen actors aren't much good at speaking in public, and so we had better just act out our thanks!

In pantomime he bows, throws a big kiss, and seems to embrace the whole audience, as there is loud applause. As Lina opens her mouth again, Don leads her off stage. (See film still 9.)

Don and Lina have just come off the stage. Cosmo is waiting in the wings with Rod, a breezy, overenergetic press-agent type, and producer Simpson.

SIMPSON: Don, Lina, you were gorgeous!

COSMO: Yes, Lina, you looked pretty good for a girl.

Lina is absolutely furious and turns on Don. We hear her voice for the first time. It is shrill, flat, and coarse, and a terrific shock coming out of that beautiful face.

LINA: F'heaven's sake, what's the idea—can't a girl get in a word in edgewise? They're my public, too!

SIMPSON *(patiently)*: But, Lina, the publicity department—Rod here—decided it would be better if Don made all the speeches for the team.

LINA: Why?

ROD: Lina, you're a beautiful woman—audience thinks you've got a voice to match. Studio has got to keep their stars from looking ridiculous, at any cost.

COSMO: No one's got that much money.

LINA: What's wrong with the way I talk? What'sa big idea—am I dumb or somethin'?

The men exchange looks.

ROD: No—it's just that Don's had so much more experience, and—

LINA: Next time, write me out a speech. I could memoralize it!

COSMO: Sure, why don't you go out now and recite the Gettysburg Address?

LINA: What do you know about it, you—you piano player! Are you anybody?! *(She turns to Don appealingly)* Don, how can you let him talk that way to me—your fiancée! *(Pronounced* fee-an-see)

DON *(clutching his head—he has been through this many times)*: My fiancée! Lina, you've been reading those fan magazines again. You actually believe that *banana oil* that Dora Bailey and all the columnists dish out. There is *nothing* between us! There has never been anything between us—just air!

LINA: *(she has been looking at him lovingly through this and now smiles at him)*: Oh, Don—you don't mean that. Come on, darling, we'll be late for Mr. Simpson's party!

ROD *(taking Lina out)*: You're going in separate cars to break up the mobs.

LINA: Ta-ta, Donny! See you there!

They exit.

DON *(looking after her, shaking his head incredulously)*: What is the *matter* with that girl? Can't she take a gentle hint?

22

COSMO: Haven't you heard? She's irresistible! She told me so herself!

DON: I can't get her out of my hair. This cooked-up romance. Just for publicity.

COSMO: The price of fame, Don! Now you've got the glory. You've got to take the little heartaches that go with it. Now, look at me. I got no glory. I got no fame. I got no big mansions. I got no money. But I've got—What have I got?

DON: I don't know. What have you got?

COSMO: I gotta get outta here.

Hollywood Boulevard

Don and Cosmo in a car, latter driving. They stop, react, and climb out of the car. People and vehicles are seen in the background.

DON: Don't tell me—it's a flat tire.

COSMO: I can't understand it. This car hasn't given me a lick of trouble in nearly six hours.

AD LIB *(from the crowd)*: Hey, there's Don Lockwood!

A group of children run forward and excitedly crowd around Don and Cosmo. (See film still 10.)

AD LIBS: Hey, gimme your autograph. Oh. Gee.

DON: Hi ya, kids.

AD LIBS: Give me your autograph, Mr. Lockwood. Gimme—I want a souvenir. I want a souvenir—I want one, too. Gimme—Gimme. Please. C'mon, gimme—

DON: Hey! Wait! Hey, Cos—do something—call me a cab!

COSMO: Okay. You're a cab.

DON: Thanks a lot.

Don's a captive of the group of young fans tugging at his jacket, pleading for autographs and souvenirs. They are about to pull it apart. One sleeve is half ripped off at the shoulder. Don calls out for help—breaks away from them and runs. He climbs up

23

on an automobile; from the automobile he climbs atop a moving trolley car. He runs to the rear of the car along the roof.

A young girl is driving her open jalopy alongside the trolley car; Don jumps down from the top of the trolley into the car, beside her. She screams.

DON: Lady, keep driving—they're after me!

KATHY SELDON *(young, pretty, and at the moment terrified)*: Huh! You get out of here!

DON: Don't stop the car, keep going!

KATHY *(driving)*: Oooh! I'll—I'll call a policeman!

DON: Don't do that. Just a few blocks and I'll get out.

KATHY: Don't hurt me!

DON: Don't worry, I'm not a criminal.

KATHY *(still very frightened)*: I don't care what you are, just go away.

DON: Now look, girlie, I'm—

KATHY *(still driving, steals a look at him and gasps)*: You *are* a criminal; I've seen that face someplace. You're a famous gangster! I've seen your picture in the papers—or in the post office with a lot of numbers on your chest.

She looks around wildly and sees a policeman at the corner.

KATHY: Officer!

She pulls over to the side.

POLICEMAN *(walking over)*: What?

KATHY *(breathless)*: Officer—this man—

POLICEMAN: What is this? What's the matter?

KATHY: This man—he's—he jumped into my car and—I don't even know who he is.

POLICEMAN *(with the light of recognition)*: Oh—why, it's Don Lockwood.

KATHY *(looking at him)*: Don Lockwood.

POLICEMAN *(warmly)*: How are you, Mr. Lockwood? Out for a joy ride?

DON: Just a lift, officer. My car broke down. I got surrounded by—

POLICEMAN: Ha-ha. You're a lucky little lady. Anything wrong?

KATHY *(pulling herself together)*: Why—why, no.

POLICEMAN *(laughing)*: I should think not. Well, good night, Mr. Lockwood.

DON: Good night, officer.

He walks on. There is a pause.

DON *(looking at the girl)*: Well—thanks for saving my life. I'll get out now.

KATHY *(recovering, but still somewhat embarrassed)*: I'm—I'm driving to Beverly Hills. Can I drop you someplace?

DON *(smiling, taking her all in)*: Well, I would like to get out of this ventilated suit if you're going by Camden and Sunset.

Kathy starts the car.

KATHY: Yes. I am.

There is a moment's silence during which Don is looking at her. He obviously finds her attractive and assumes an ingratiating manner.

DON: I'd very much like to know whose hospitality I'm enjoying.

KATHY: Selden—Kathy Selden.

DON: Enchanted, Miss Selden. I'm sorry I frightened you—I was getting just a little too much love from my adoring fans.

KATHY *(noticing his torn coat for the first time)*: Oh—that's what you were running away from. They did that to you? . . . That's terrible.

DON *(moving a little closer to her)*: Yes, yes, it is, isn't it? It is terrible. Well, we movie stars get the glory—I guess we have to take the little heartaches that go with it. People think we lead lives of glamour and romance, but we're really lonely. Terribly lonely.

His arm is now draped over the back of the driver's seat in back of her.

KATHY *(obviously annoyed by his line and assuming an overly sweet gaga manner)*: Uh—Mr. Lockwood—I can't tell you how sorry I am about taking you for a criminal before, but it was understandable under the circumstances. . . .

DON: Sure.

KATHY: I knew I'd seen you.

DON: Which of my pictures have you seen?

KATHY: I don't remember. I saw one once.

DON: You saw one once?

KATHY (*in the same overinnocent vein*): Yes, I think you were dueling, and there was a girl—Lina Lamont. No, I don't go to the movies much. If you've seen one, you've seen them all.

DON (*stung*): Oh, thank you.

KATHY: Oh, no offense. Movies are entertaining enough for the masses, but the personalities on the screen just don't impress me. I mean, they don't talk—they . . . don't act—they just make a lot of dumb show. Well, you know—like that.

She does a silent-movie pantomime.

DON: You mean—like what I do?

KATHY: Well, yes. Here we are, Sunset and Camden!

She stops the car.

DON: Wait a minute. You mean I'm not an actor—pantomime on the screen isn't acting.

KATHY: Well, of course not. Acting means great parts, wonderful lines—speaking those glorious words.

DON: Words?

KATHY: Shakespeare—Ibsen—

DON: Tell me, what's your lofty mission in life that lets you sneer at my humble profession?

KATHY (*suddenly confused*): Well, I'm—I'm an actress.

DON: What?

KATHY: On the stage.

DON: Oh, on the stage. Well, I'd like to see you act. What're you in right now? I could brush up on my English, or bring along an interpreter. That is, if they'd let in a movie actor.

KATHY: Well, I'm not in a play right now, but I will be. I'm going to New York, and I'm—

DON: Oh, you're going to New York, and then someday we'll all hear of you, won't we? Kathy Selden as Juliet, as Lady Macbeth, as King Lear—you'll have to wear a beard for that one, of course—

KATHY: Oh, you can laugh if you want to, but at least the stage is a dignified profession.

DON: Dignified!

KATHY: And what have you got to be so conceited about? You're nothing but a shadow on film—a shadow—you're not flesh and blood.

DON *(leaning toward her, leering)*: Oh, no?

KATHY *(pulling back)*: Stop!

DON: What could I do to you? I'm only a shadow.

KATHY *(defiant)*: You keep away from me. Just because you're a big movie star—wild parties—swimming pools—you expect every girl to fall in a dead faint at your feet. Well, don't you touch me.

DON *(getting out, slamming the door)*: Fear not, sweet Lady— I will not molest you. I am but a humble jester, and you—you are too far above me. Farewell, Ethel Barrymore, I must tear myself from your side!

He has caught the tail of his torn coat in the door, and as he leaves, it rips to shreds. Kathy laughs and drives off. (See film still 11.)

Driveway of Simpson's Mansion

Kathy drives in.

KATHY: Hello, is this R. F. Simpson's house?

BUTLER: Yes, miss.

KATHY: Well, I'm one of the girls from the Coconut Grove.

BUTLER: Ah, yes—the floor show—around the back, please.

KATHY: Oh, I see. Thank you.

Simpson's Living Room

A huge Hollywood living room, furnished in late 1920's style. A big party is in progress and we see, dancing an exaggerated tango, several couples, including Zelda Zanders and Olga Mara and other movie types. Lina is there, surrounded by adoring men, all offering to light her cigarette. In a reckless, grand gesture, she flings the cigarette up over her head. Dexter and Simpson are moving through the guests. Cosmo is with a girl.

DEXTER: Nice little party, R. F.

SIMPSON: Thanks, Roscoe.

GIRL: Oh, Mr. Brown, do you really think you could get me in the movies?

COSMO *(being the big shot)*: Oh, I think so.

GIRL: Really?

We see Don entering, being surrounded by people offering congratulations. Cosmo joins him.

COSMO: Don? How did you come, by way of Australia?

DON *(very seriously)*: Hello, Cos. Say, listen, Cos—tell me the truth. Am I a good actor?

COSMO: Well, as long as I'm working for Monumental Pictures, you're the greatest of them all.

DON: Now, no kidding, Cos—you're my pal—you can tell me.

COSMO: What's the matter with you? Of course, you're good.

DON: Well, maybe you'd better keep telling me from time to time. I feel a little shaken.

COSMO: The new Don Lockwood.

SIMPSON: Don!

DON: Oh, hi, R. F.

SIMPSON: Don, it's colossal. Where have you been? We've been waiting for you. Been holding the show for you.

LINA *(taking his arm)*: There you are, Donny. Where have you been? I was lonely.

DON *(wearily)*: Hello, Lina.

28

SIMPSON *(holding Don and Lina by the arm, to the guests)*: Okay, fellas, hold it. Together again, my two little stars. Don and Lina. No kidding, folks, aren't they great? All right, open that screen.

DON: A movie? We've just seen one.

COSMO: You gotta show a movie at a party—it's a Hollywood law.

SIMPSON: Listen, everybody, I've got a few little surprises for you tonight. All right, everyone—sit down—sit down. Listen, this is going to hand you a lot of laughs. There's a madman coming into my office now for months, and, well—

> *People sit on the floor. A movie screen is lowered, lights dim, and movie screen lights up.*

SIMPSON: You got that gadget working, Sam?

SAM: All set, Mr. Simpson.

SIMPSON: Okay. Let 'er go.

> *The screen is blank for a moment. Suddenly there is a strange hissing sound seemingly coming from behind the screen. We see on the screen a nondescript professorial-looking man at a desk, who shuffles several papers which sound like a thunderstorm. The film is in very flat, crude black and white.*

MAN ON SCREEN *(speaking very loudly but with a voice full of echoes—also very deliberately, as one who overelaborately forms words for a deaf person)*: This is a demonstration of a talking picture. Notice—it is a picture of me—and I am talking! Note how my lips and the sound issuing from them are synchronized together in perfect unison.

GIRL: Who's that?

MAN: There's someone talking behind the screen.

A GIRL: Come out from behind that screen, Mr. Simpson.

SIMPSON *(laughing)*: No, no—I'm right here!

MAN ON SCREEN *(continuing)*: Since the earliest days of the cinema screen, the concept of simultaneous sound has been the primary object of our pioneer inventors. My voice has been recorded on a record. A talking picture. Thank you. Good-bye.

Man on screen smiles and nods several times in farewell, uncertain as to whether he is still on camera or not. Then the screen goes blank, and the lights in the living room come up. There is a moment's silence.

SIMPSON: Well?

MAN: Just a toy.

FIRST GIRL: It's a scream.

SECOND GIRL: It's vulgar.

SECOND MAN: R. F., do you think they'll ever really use it?

SIMPSON: I doubt it. The Warner Brothers are making a whole talking picture with this gadget—*The Jazz Singer.* They'll lose their shirts. What do you think of it, Dexter?

DEXTER: It'll never amount to a thing.

COSMO: Yeah, that's what they said about the horseless carriage.

SIMPSON: Well, let's get on with the show. Okay, boys. Come on, my little starlets. *(Takes Don and Lina through the arms and turns them around)*

A huge cake has been wheeled into the room by two chefs, and Don and Lina are facing it. The cake has the Monumental Pictures emblem on top.

SIMPSON: I have a delicious surprise. It's a very special cake. I want you kiddies to have the first piece.

As Don is looking up at the cake, a figure pops up through the center of it, a showgirl in a pink, leggy dancing outfit, with arms upstretched and a big smile expressive of "Wheeee" on her face. It is Kathy. (See film still 12.) Her look changes to one of amazement as she finds herself staring into Don's face. He looks equally amazed, then bursts into laughter.

DON: Well, if it isn't Ethel Barrymore!

Kathy steps down from the cake, in great embarrassment, as a dozen or so fellow dancing girls wearing the same outfit troop into the room to gay, blaring music from the band. Kathy and the girls walk around the room, handing out rolls of con-

30

fetti to the guests, with Don following her, now highly amused, while she tries vainly to make believe he isn't there.

DON: I do hope you're going to favor us with something special tonight.

KATHY: Please.

DON: Say . . . uh . . . Hamlet's soliloquy, or . . . or the balcony scene from *Romeo and Juliet*.

KATHY: Mr. Lockwood—

DON: Shhh—don't be shy. You'd make about the prettiest Juliet I've ever seen. Really.

Kathy and her fellow showgirls get into formation and do a lively and vivacious song-and-dance rendition of "All I Do Is Dream of You," (see film still 13) while Don stands by watching Kathy, simultaneously amused and charmed by her and her very professional show-biz skill. As the number finishes and the girls exit, Don stands in front of Kathy and detains her.

DON: I just had to tell you how good you were.

KATHY *(trying to leave)*: Excuse me.

DON *(pointing to cake)*: Oh, now, now, don't go. Now that I know where you live, I'd like to see you home.

KATHY *(angrily)*: Now, listen, Mr. Lockwood—

LINA *(coming over, suspiciously)*: Say, who's this dame, anyway?

DON *(hammily)*: Oh, someone lofty and far above us all. She couldn't learn anything from the movies. She's an actress on the legitimate stage.

KATHY *(enraged and beside herself)*: Here's one thing I've learned from the movies!

She picks up a large cake from the table and hurls it at Don, who ducks; the cake lands full in Lina's face, obliterating it in a giant pink-and-white creamy mess. There is a second of aghast silence. (See film stills 14, 15.)

LINA *(moaning from somewhere behind the whipped cream)*: Oh—oh—ohhhhhh—

KATHY *(appalled)*: Oh, Lina—

DON: Lina—

LINA *(a shrill scream)*: Let me at her—I'll kill her—I'll kill her.

> *Kathy dashes out of the room.*

DON *(trying to take some cake off Lina's dress)*: Now, Lina—
Lina—she was aiming at me.

COSMO *(who has just entered the scene)*: Lina, you've never looked
lovelier.

DON: Lina, it was just a little accident.

COSMO: Sure, it happens to me five or six times a day.

DON *(suddenly noticing Kathy is gone)*: Well, where is she?

> *He runs out after her.*

LINA *(wistfully, from behind a wall of cake)*: Donnie?

Girls' Dressing Room

> *Don dashes into the girls' dressing room, causing instant flut-
> tering hearts among the girls, who are in varied states of attire,
> midway between costume and street clothes.*

DON: Oh, excuse me—uh—where'd Miss Selden go?

GIRL: She just grabbed her things and bolted. Anything I can do?

DON: I'm sorry. I don't have the time to find out. *(He leaves,
hurriedly, by the door to the outside)*

Front of Mr. Simpson's House

> *Don comes running down the front steps in the moonlight
> just in time to see Kathy, in her little car, driving off.*

DON: Kathy! Hey, Kathy! Hey!

> *He looks down the driveway, disappointedly. Then he begins
> to smile, just at the thought of her, as he walks slowly away
> from the house.*

Gates of Monumental Pictures Studio

The entrance to a movie studio is seen in the California daylight, with the bustle of people busily walking about behind the opened gates, and a sign over the entrance, reading MONUMENTAL PICTURES.

Inside the Studio

A giant silent-movie stage is in the midst of its frenzied, normal daily activities, with several different pictures being shot at once, amidst a flow of technicians, property men, and actors dressed in many different, unrelated kinds of attire of all ages and countries—and the constant shouting of directors urging on the performers heard from all over. In one corner an African epic is being shot, with cameras trained on a jungle scene with cannibals dancing around a boiling kettle and the director shouting as they dance.

DIRECTOR: Now, keep that action going. Come on, let's go. Let's have more steam in the kettle. A little more action, boys. And a little more rhythm, boys. More steam and more water in that kettle, boys.

Don enters, on his way to the set of his new picture. He is dressed in a golfing outfit—knickered tweed suit and cap, with argyle socks—and he pauses to speak to a savage-looking off-camera cannibal.

DON: Hi ya, Maxie.

MAXIE: Hi ya, Don.

Don continues to walk, then stops as he comes upon Cosmo and a second cannibal, who is seated on a bench, munching a sandwich and reading Variety.

DON: Good morning, fellas.

COSMO: Oh, hi ya, Don.

SECOND CANNIBAL: Hi ya.

COSMO: Hey, did you read *Variety* today? "First talking picture novelty—*The Jazz Singer*—all-time smash end of first week."

SECOND CANNIBAL: All-time flop end of the second.

DON: Well, we start today.

SECOND CANNIBAL: Good luck.

DON: Thanks. I am now Comte Pierre de Battaille—better known as the Dueling Cavalier.

COSMO: Yeah? What's this one about?

DON: It's a French Revolution story.

COSMO: Don't tell me. You're a French aristocrat, and she's a simple girl of the people—and she won't even give you a tumbril. Ahh.

DON: Well, it's a living.

> *Cosmo and Don start walking past other sets. They pass two men fighting on top of a train with a moving canvas background.*

COSMO: Good morning.

MAN: Hi.

DIRECTOR *(shouting toward train)*: Say, now, keep that background moving. Hit him. Hit him. Come on. Knock him down. Get up there. Hit him again. Hurry up. Hit that man down.

COSMO *(to Don)*: Hey, why bother to shoot the picture? Why don't you release the old one under a new title? If you've seen one, you've seen them all.

DON *(sharply)*: Hey . . . why'd you say that for?

COSMO: What's the matter?

DON *(brooding)*: That's what that Kathy Selden said to me that night.

COSMO: That's three weeks ago. You still thinking about that?

DON: Well, I can't get her out of my mind.

COSMO: How could you? She's the first dame who hasn't fallen for your line since you were four.

DON: I guess she's on my conscience.

COSMO: It's not your fault she lost her job at the Grove.

34

DON (*very concerned*): Anyway, I've got to find her.

COSMO: Well, you've been trying to, haven't you? Short of sending out bloodhounds and a posse?

DON: I suppose so.

COSMO: Come on, now—snap out of it. You can't let a little thing like this get you down. Why, you're Don Lockwood, aren't you? And Don Lockwood's an actor, isn't he? Well, what's the first thing an actor learns? The show must go on. Come rain, come shine, come snow, come sleet—the show must go on. So *ridi*, Pagliacci, *ridi*.

DON: *Ridi*, huh?

COSMO: Yeah.

Cosmo sits down at a piano and plays as he talks.

COSMO: Don, the world is so full of a number of things. I'm sure we should all be as happy as— But are we? No. Definitely no. Positively no. (*He punctuates this with chords*) Decidedly no. Uh-uh. Short people have long faces, and long people have short faces. Big people have little humor, and little people have no humor at all.

Don is watching, amused, from a chair.

And in the words of that immortal bard, Samuel J. Snodgrass, as he was about to be led to the guillotine—

Cosmo sings and dances "Make 'Em Laugh."

In the course of this number, Cosmo executes many wildly surrealistic comic bits, in a style that combines a feeling of easy improvisation with violence. He is smashed in the face, walking into a large plank being carried by workmen; he opens a door that he expects to lead to some other room and walks nose-on into a brick wall; he has a short flirtation, followed by a ferocious fight, with a headless cloth dummy, all manipulated by him; and he runs acrobatically up several walls with scenes of hallways painted on them, and back-flips off them, finally leaping against one wall that turns out to have no backing. He hurtles through it, rending a large hole in it, through which

*he re-emerges, battered, sings an ending to "Make 'Em Laugh,"
and collapses.*

Set of *The Dueling Cavalier*
*A formal French garden, with a marble bench, bushes, and
hedges. Near it are several portable dressing rooms, and a setup
of cameras, lights, etc. Dexter, the director, megaphone in
hand, knocks on a dressing room door which reads* DON
LOCKWOOD.

DEXTER: Ready, Don?

DON *(emerging, dressed in elegant eighteenth-century attire with
white wig, a courtly male figure)*: All set, Roscoe.

DEXTER *(enthusiastically)*: Well, here we go again. I think we
have another smash on our hands.

DON: I hope so.

DEXTER: You're darn tootin' we have. Where's Lina?

WOMAN: Here she is, Mr. Dexter.

DEXTER: Well, well. Here comes our lovely leading lady now.

*Lina enters, flanked by a hairdresser and wardrobe woman,
and looking breathtakingly beautiful and aristocratic in her
huge bouffant eighteenth-century skirt and bare bodice and
high, towering, powdered wig. Her voice sounds more ludicrous
than ever, by contrast.*

LINA *(testily)*: Gee, this wig weighs a ton. What dope'll wear a
thing like this?

DEXTER: Everybody used to wear them, Lina.

LINA: Well, then, everybody was a dope.

WOMAN: Honey, you look just beautiful.

DEXTER: Yes, you look great. Let's get into the set.

A workman hands a courtier's staff to Don.

DON: Thanks, Joe.

Don walks over to garden set, and is joined by Lina, who sits

36

5

6

7

8

12

13

14

15

16

17

18

19

20

21

22

23

28

29

30

31

32

33

34

35

36

37

38

39

40

41

42

43

44

45

46

on the bench, and talks to him while set dressers and lighting technicians are finishing their work for shooting.

LINA: I looked for you the other night at Wally Ray's party. Where were you?

DON: Oh, I've been busy.

DEXTER: Give us the lights, Sam.

LINA *(nastily edgy)*: And I know what you've been busy at—lookin' for that girl.

DON: As a matter of fact, yes.

LINA: Why—

DON: I've been worried about her.

LINA: Yeah? Well, you should've been worried about me a little. After all, I'm the one who got the whipped cream in a kisser.

DON: Yes, but you didn't lose your job, and she did.

LINA *(triumphantly)*: You darned tootin' she did. I arranged it.

DON *(shocked)*: What?

LINA: Well, they weren't gonna fire her, so I called 'em up and told them they'd better.

DEXTER: Okay, Don. Now, remember. You're madly in love with her.

DON *(jaw set, ready to kill her)*: Ummmmm—

DEXTER: And you have to overcome her shyness and timidity.

Don, seething with anger, exits upstage side of the garden set. Cosmo, mood music!

Cosmo, at the piano, starts playing the stately minuet from Mozart's Don Giovanni, *which continues through the shooting of the love scene.*

ROLL 'EM! ! !

This is the big moment on any set. Workman enters with slate, on which is written name of picture, director, scene number, and date, and holds it in front of camera. Lina's hairdresser does some last-second adjusting on her wig, and then runs off. The workman exits with the slate, and—

Okay, Don. Now enter.

Don enters the set, with romance in his eyes, looking for his love.

You see her! Run to her!

Don sees Lina, sitting there pensively and sadly, does an ecstatic take, throws his staff away, and rushes forward to her. He puts his hands over her eyes, her shoulders lift in happy recognition, and as he removes his hands, they gaze at each other with the purest of love shining in their eyes. The spoken exchanges that follow between them take place against the silent, tender love scene that they are playing for the camera. (See film stills 16, 17, 18.)

DON *(in grim tones, over his lover's smile)*: Why, you rattlesnake, you. You got that poor kid fired.

LINA *(equally smiling)*: That's not all I'm gonna do if I ever get my hands on her.

DON: I never heard of anything so low.

DEXTER *(glowing)*: Fine. Fine. Looks great.

DON *(kneeling beside her)*: What did you do it for?

LINA *(tapping him lightly on the shoulder with her fan)*: 'Cause you liked her. I could tell.

DON *(takes her arm and kisses her hand)*: So that's it. Believe me, I don't like her half as much as I hate you. You reptile!

LINA: Sticks and stones may break my bones—

DON *(rising)*: I'd like to break every bone in your body.

LINA *(rising)*: You and who else—you big lummox!

DEXTER: Now, kiss her, Don.

Don and Lina kiss passionately.

DEXTER *(excitedly)*: That's it. More. Great. Cut.

They break from the kiss, Don turning away in open disgust.

LINA *(breathlessly)*: Oh, Donny. You couldn't kiss me like that and not mean it just a teensy-weensy bit.

DON: Meet the greatest actor in the world. I'd rather kiss a tarantula.

LINA *(smiling)*: Ahhhh—you don't mean that.

DON: I don't? Hey, Joe, bring me a tarantula. Now, listen, Lina—

DEXTER: Stop that chit-chat, you love birds. Let's get another take.

SIMPSON *(entering)*: Hold it. Hold it, Dexter.

DEXTER *(cheerily)*: Hello, Mr. Simpson. We're really rolling.

SIMPSON *(very grim)*: Yeah, well, you can stop rolling at once.

DEXTER: Huh?

SIMPSON *(calling his stars to his side)*: Don—Lina.

DEXTER *(to the crew)*: All right, everybody, save it!

SIMPSON: Save it? Tell them to go home. We're shutting down for a few weeks.

DEXTER *(stunned)*: What?

SIMPSON: Well, don't just stand there. Tell them.

DEXTER *(his not to reason why)*: Everybody go home until further notice. *(To Simpson)* What is this?

DON: Yeah, what's the matter, R. F.?

SIMPSON: *The Jazz Singer*, that's what's the matter. *The Jazz Singer*.

COSMO *(jumping to the piano and singing)*:

> Oh, my darling little mammy
> Down in Alabamy
> I'm your little baby—

SIMPSON *(cutting him off)*: This is no joke, Cosmo. It's a sensation. The public is screaming for more.

DON: More what?

SIMPSON: Talking pictures—talking pictures.

DON: Ah, it's just a freak.

SIMPSON *(angrily)*: Yeah, what a freak! We should have such a freak at this studio. I told you talking pictures were a menace, but no one would listen to me. Don, we're going to put our best feet forward. We're going to make *The Dueling Cavalier* into a talking picture.

COSMO: Talking picture? Why, that means I'm out of a job. At last I can start suffering and write that symphony.

SIMPSON: You're not out of a job. We're putting you in as head of the new music department.

COSMO *(shaking his hand)*: Well, thanks, R. F. At last I can stop suffering and write that symphony.

DEXTER *(bewildered)*: Now, wait a second, Mr. Simpson. Talking pictures. I think you should wait—

SIMPSON: Every studio is jumping on the band wagon, Dexter. All the theaters are putting in sound equipment. We don't want to be left out of it.

DON: But we don't know anything about this gadget.

SIMPSON: What do you have to know? It's a picture. You do what you always did. You just add talking to it.

DON *(worried)*: Yeah?

SIMPSON: Don, believe me, it will be a sensation. Lamont and Lockwood. They talk.

LINA *(in her coarsest, flattest tones, cutting through like a knife)*: Well, of course we talk. Don't *i*verybody?

After a silence, Dexter, Simpson, and Don turn and look at her, then exchange a bewildered look.

Series of Headlines

These are all front pages of Variety, *and they each spin forward from a great distance and end up smack in front of our eyes.*

VARIETY

REVOLUTION IN HOLLYWOOD
Execs A-Dither
at Pic Sound

VARIETY

STUDIOS CONVERT TO TALKIES
Mad Scramble
on for Sound

40

This is followed by a montage, which shows, in rapid succession, bits of typical musical numbers in the style of vintage 1929–1930 film musicals. We see first a trio of singing girls, with overeager expressions, who are scat-singing, "Vo-do-do-dee-oh" style; then a shot of dancing girls with cocktail shakers cavorting while balloons fall around them, as off-screen we hear the sung strains of "I've Got a Feelin' You're Foolin'." This is followed by another line of dancing girls, made up as dolls, wearing sentinel outfits, doing a puppetlike military drill to "The Wedding of the Painted Doll." Next there is a shot of a man, strongly resembling Rudy Vallee, singing "Should I Reveal Exactly How I Feel" nasally and plaintively into a megaphone, followed by a boy-girl collegiate couple, prancing along to another riff accompaniment. There is an accelerated intercutting of all these separate numbers, as the montage reaches a hectic climax, then goes to a final shot of the singing girl trio, who slow down their "Vo-do-dee-oh's" into the stately tempo of "Beautiful Girl."

A Stage at Monumental Studios

A production number is being photographed. A juvenile-lead type in straw hat and cane and beach blazer is singing "Beautiful Girl," surrounded by dancing girls in long, summery outfits, with large hats and parasols. (See film still 19.) One of the girls is Kathy. Watching the number being shot are Cosmo, Simpson, and Zelda Zanders, all standing very near the camera and crew. Simpson is eyeing Kathy.

41

SIMPSON *(aside, to a man next to him)*: Who's that little girl on the right? She looks familiar.

PHILLIPS *(the dance director)*: I meant to talk to you about her. I've featured her before in lots of nightclub shows.

SIMPSON: That's probably where I've seen her.

PHILLIPS: She'd be very good in the part of Zelda's kid sister.

SIMPSON: That's a good idea.

COSMO *(recognizing Kathy)*: Excuse me. *(He dashes out)*
> *The number continues, with a late-twenties fashion show featuring lovely ladies in many kinds of attire: the four seasons, a wedding, widow's weeds, sports—seen one by one with terribly coy accompanying spoken couplets recited by the singing juvenile, and the number is climaxed with a pioneering, pre-Busby Berkeley overhead shot of the juvenile and the girls dancing in a circle, staring upward as it comes to an end.*

SIMPSON *(visibly moved)*: That's stupendous.

PHILLIPS: Thanks. Kathy—come here a minute, will you, please?

SIMPSON: This'll start a new trend in musical pictures.

PHILLIPS *(as she joins them)*: Kathy, this is Mr. Simpson. He's thinking about casting you as Zelda's kid sister.

KATHY *(enthusiastically)*: Oh, that's wonderful, Mr. Simpson.

DON *(entering with Cosmo and excitedly joining the group)*: Hey, Kathy! That's Kathy Selden.

KATHY *(resignedly, to Simpson)*: Well, thanks anyway, it was nice of you.

SIMPSON: Now, wait a minute—what—

KATHY: Oh, that's all right, Mr. Simpson—and before Mr. Lockwood refreshes your memory, you might as well know. I'm the girl who hit Miss Lamont with the cake. Believe me, it was meant for Mr. Lockwood. *(To Phillips)* Good-bye, Sid—I'm sorry—I should have told you. *(She starts to leave)*

DON: Wait a minute, Miss Selden. What's this all about, R. F.?

SIMPSON: Well, we were going to use Miss Selden in Zelda's picture, but if it would make you and Lina unhappy—

42

DON (looking at Kathy): Unhappy? I think it's wonderful.

COSMO: Sure. He's been looking for her for weeks.

SIMPSON (nervously): Are you speaking for Lina also?

DON: Now, look, R. F., the owner of the Coconut Grove may do what Lina tells him to, but you're the head of this studio.

SIMPSON (firmly): Yes, I'm the head of this studio. She's hired, but don't let Lina know she's on the lot. That's settled. Take care of that, Phillips. (He exits)

KATHY (overjoyed): Oh, thank you, Mr. Simpson.

COSMO (to Kathy): Gee, I'm glad you turned up. We've been looking inside every cake in town.

On the Movie Lot

Kathy and Don stroll down the lot, past several sound stages, as they talk. It's a lovely afternoon, and Don is obviously terribly happy at having found her.

KATHY (as they walk): Is it all right for you to be seen publicly with me?

DON: You mean lofty star with humble player?

KATHY: Not exactly. But for lunch, don't you usually tear a pheasant with Miss Lamont?

DON: Oh, now look, Kathy, all that stuff about Lina and me is sheer publicity.

KATHY: Oh. Certainly seems more than that, from what I've read in the columns and all those articles in the fan magazines.

DON (catching her up): Oh? You read the fan magazines?

KATHY (trying to get out of it): Well, I—I pick them up in the beauty parlor, or the dentist's office. Just like anybody.

DON: Honest?

KATHY (shamefacedly): Well, I buy four or five a month.

DON: You buy four or five—

KATHY (completely flustered): Well, anyway—to get back to the main point—

43

DON: Yes?

KATHY: You and Miss Lamont do achieve a kind of intimacy in all your pictures that would—

DON (*catching her again*): Did you say *all* my pictures?

KATHY: I guess now that I think of it, I've seen eight or nine of them.

DON: Eight or nine. You know, it seems to me I remember someone saying, "If you've seen one, you've seen 'em all."

KATHY (*laughing*): I did say some awful things that night, didn't I?

DON (*simply*): No. I deserved them. Of course, I must admit I was pretty much upset by 'em. So upset that I haven't been able to think of anything but you ever since.

KATHY (*really taken aback*): Honest?

DON: Honest.

KATHY: Well, I've been pretty upset, too.

DON (*suddenly shy, boyish*): Kathy. Kathy, look, I—Kathy, seeing you again, now that I—Kathy, I'm trying to say something to you, but I . . . I'm such a ham. I guess I'm not able to, without the proper setting.

KATHY: What do you mean?

DON (*taking her by the hand*): Well . . . C'mere.

They are in front of the large door of one of the big stages. He pulls it open, and they walk onto the dark studio floor, empty except for some stray props and working equipment.

DON: This is the proper setting.

KATHY: Why, it's just an empty stage.

DON: At first glance—yes. But wait a second.

He goes over to a light switchboard and starts pulling levers down. The stage is gradually flooded with shafts of light, creating an atmosphere of outdoors, a soft, rosy evening glow.

A beautiful sunset. Mist from the distant mountains.

He pulls another switch that floods the stage in a soft, misty haze.

Colored lights in a garden.

He pulls more light switches, and stronger beams of light of several colors spill around them. Holding hands, he leads her to a ladder, and she climbs several steps.

A lady is standing in her balcony in a rose-trellised bower, flooded with moonlight. We add five hundred thousand kilowatts of stardust.

He switches a large spotlight on Kathy. Then he turns on a wind machine that sweeps gently over Kathy, completing a total atmosphere of romance around them, with Don standing looking up at her on the ladder.

A soft summer breeze—and—you sure look lovely in the moonlight, Kathy.

KATHY: Now that you have the proper setting, can you say it?

DON: I'll try.

He sings "You Were Meant for Me" to her, and they do a tender dance together, old-fashioned and unaffected, and end with him lifting her back onto the ladder and standing beside her with love in his eyes. (See film still 20.)

Front page of *Variety*:

HOLLYWOOD LEARNS TO TALK

Big Bonanza for Diction Coaches

Exterior office door with lettering which reads:

DICTION COACH

Phoebe Dinsmore

Interior Dinsmore Office

Lina and Phoebe Dinsmore are engaged in an elocution lesson.

MISS DINSMORE *(a buxom, grand lady, concealing her impatience with fortitude)*: Now! Ta-tay-tee-toe-too.

LINA (*impossibly nasal and flat, but totally unaware of anything wrong*): Ta-tay-tee-toe-too.

MISS DINSMORE: No, no, Miss Lamont. Rrround tones. Rrround tones. Now, let me hear you rrread your line.

LINA (*very flat on the "an" sounds*): "And I can't *stan'* 'im."

MISS DINSMORE: "And I cahn't *stand* him."

LINA: "And I can't *stan'* 'im."

MISS DINSMORE: "Cahn't!"

LINA: "Can't."

MISS DINSMORE: "Caaahn't!"

LINA (*a goat bleating*): "Caaaan't."

Interior Diction Coach's Office

Don, dressed casually in open-necked sweater and slacks, is being coached by a professorial-looking male diction teacher. Don is obviously having very little trouble.

DON: "Cahn't. Cahn't."

TEACHER (*reading from book*): Very good. Now. "Around the rocks the rugged rascal ran."

DON: "Around the rocks the rugged—"

TEACHER: No. No. "Rrrocks—Rrrocks."

DON: "Around the rocks the rugged rascal ran." Hi, Cos.

TEACHER: Very good.

COSMO (*who has just entered*): Oh, hi, Don.

TEACHER (*not liking being interrupted*): Shall I continue?

DON: Yeah, go ahead.

COSMO (*cheerfully*): Don't mind me.

TEACHER: Now. "Sinful Caesar sipped his snifter, seized his knees, and sneezed."

DON: "Sinful Caesar snipped his sifter—"

TEACHER: No, no. "Sipped his snifter."

COSMO (*echoing the teacher*): "Sipped his snifter."

46

DON: Oh, thank you. "Sinful Caesar sipped his snifter, seized his knees, and sneezed."

TEACHER: Marvelous.

COSMO *(condescendingly)*: Wonderful.

TEACHER: Marvelous! Oh—Oh, here is a good one. Uh—"Chester chooses chestnuts, cheddar cheese, with chewy chives. He chews them and he chooses them—he chooses them and he chews them—those chestnuts, cheddar cheese, and chives in cheery charming chunks."

COSMO *(applauding, in mock admiration)*: Wonderful—do another one.

TEACHER *(flattered)*: Oh, thank you. *(Then, proudly)* "Moses supposes his toeses are roses, but Moses supposes erroneously—Moses he knowses his toeses aren't roses as Moses supposes his toeses to be."

During this tongue-twister, Cosmo apes the teacher's speech along with him, doing wild distorted expressions, which he manages to check every time the teacher glances at him, but Cosmo's timing is off at the finish and he is suddenly staring straight at the teacher with an all-out gargoyle look. Flustered, the teacher hands the book he has been reading from to Don, who reads.

DON: "Moses supposes his toeses are roses, but Moses supposes erroneously."

Cosmo picks up reciting the tongue-twister, but in rhythm, and Don and he continue in song and dance—"Moses." As Don throws the book in the air, they tap-dance around the teacher, who is taken aback, as they escort him out of the way by the ends of his tie. The dance is vigorous, precise, and athletic. The number ends as they seat the reluctant teacher on top of the desk and pile everything movable in the room on top of him—a chair across his lap, drapes over his head, lamp shade, pillow, wastebasket, etc., and finally Don takes a sign

47

off the wall that reads VOWEL A *and places it over all the other objects. They finish their dance, point to the sign, and and loudly sing.*

COSMO AND DON: "A"! *(See film stills 21, 22, 23, 24.)*

Interior Sound Stage

On the door inside the sound stage there is a sign which reads:

QUIET WHILE
RECORDING

The air is filled with tension in the face of the unknown. The talkie edition of The Dueling Cavalier *is being filmed, and we are back in the garden set, but it's not the same. The floor is strewn everywhere with wiring and cables for the sound, and there are lots more people around, sound men, several assistant directors, electricians, diction coaches, etc. Roscoe Dexter, the director, is suddenly a man unsure of himself. Still neatly capped and putteed, but without the security of the familiar megaphone to shout through, he is a nervous wreck trying hard to control himself.*

DEXTER *(patiently)*: All right, here we go. Quiet!

FIRST ASSISTANT DIRECTOR: Quiet!

SECOND ASSISTANT DIRECTOR: Quiet!

DEXTER: Roll 'em!

Interior Recording Booth

Dexter enters door, closes it carefully, and sits beside sound engineers, who are seated at a control board wearing earphones. Dexter is enclosed, separated from the actors outside. Through the glass partition he can see Don and Lina doing the love scene at the bench in their eighteenth-century attire, and Lina is speaking.

LINA *(barely audible)*: "Oh, Pierre, you shouldn't have come. You're—"

SOUND ENGINEER *(to Dexter)*: She's got to talk into the mike. I can't pick it up.

Dexter gets up and walks out onto the set.

DEXTER: Cut!

DON *(eager to please)*: What's the matter, Dexter?

DEXTER *(with great control)*: Lina, look, Lina, don't you remember? I told you. There's a microphone right there—in the bush.

He lifts a bulky round microphone out of the bush and shows it to Lina.

LINA *(disgusted)*: Yeah.

DEXTER: You have to talk into it.

LINA *(turning to Miss Dinsmore, who is nearby)*: I was talking, wasn't I, Miss Dinsmore?

MISS DINSMORE: Yes, my dear, but please remember—round tones. "Pierre, you shouldn't have come."

LINA *(as nasally as ever)*: "Pierre, you shouldn't have come."

MISS DINSMORE: Yes, yes, my dear, that's much better. Now—

DEXTER: Hold it a second. Now, Lina, look, here's the mike. Right here in the bush.

LINA: Yeah.

DEXTER *(very carefully, emphasizing every word, but near the breaking point)*: Now, you talk to it. The sound goes through the cable to the box. A man records it on a big record in wax, but you have to talk into the mike *first—in the bush*. Now, try it again. *(See film still 25.)*

LINA: Gee, this is dumb.

DON *(edgy, too, but trying to be on top of it)*: Oh, she'll get it, Dexter. Look, Lina, don't worry, we're all a little nervous the first day. Everything's going to be okay. Oh, by the way, Roscoe, you know the scene coming up, where I say, "Imperious princess of

49

the night"? I—I don't like those lines there. Is . . . is it all right if I just say what I always do. "I . . . I love you—I love you—I love you."

DEXTER: Sure. Any way it's comfortable. But into the bush. Okay. Again. Quiet.

FIRST ASSISTANT: Quiet!

SECOND ASSISTANT: Quiet!

DEXTER *(wearily)*: Roll 'em.

Interior Recording Booth

Dexter enters and sits beside sound engineer; Don and Lina seen through glass partition. Lina speaks.

LINA *(moving her head from side to side so that the mike fails to pick up every other word or so)*: "Pi——shou——come!"

Dexter gets up in a panic and runs back out to the set.

DEXTER: Cut! Lina, we're missing every other word. You've got to talk into the mike.

LINA *(exploding)*: Well, I can't make love to a *bush!*

DEXTER *(half to himself, desperately)*: All right. All right. We'll have to think of something else.

On Set

A wardrobe woman is finishing sewing a corsage to the center of the bosom of Lina's dress.

LINA: What are you doing?

WARDROBE WOMAN: You're being wired for sound, honey.

LINA: What?

MISS DINSMORE: Now, remember, Miss Lamont, watch out for those dentalized "d's" and "t's" and those flat "a's."

LINA: Everybody's picking on me.

DEXTER: Okay, Lina, now look at this flower, see? *(He points to corsage)* The mike is in there. That's it. Now, the sound will run from it, through this wire, onto the record. It'll catch whatever you say.

We see that the wire goes down inside Lina's dress and out the bottom of her skirt onto the floor.

Now, let's hear how it sounds, Lina. Okay—Quiet!

FIRST ASSISTANT: Quiet!

SECOND ASSISTANT: Quiet!

DEXTER *(looking up to heaven)*: Roll 'em!

Dexter enters the recording booth, and sits, looking through glass at Don and Lina. Lina starts her line, and through the whole thing we hear a loud, thumping sound, like the drums of doom.

LINA *(muffled by thumping)*: "Oh, Pierre, you shouldn't have come. You are flirting with danger. You—"

DEXTER: What's that noise?

ENGINEER: The mike's picking up her heartbeat.

DEXTER: Swell. Cut!

On Set

The wardrobe woman is now sewing the corsage on Lina's shoulder. The wire still runs inside the neck of her dress and down under her dress to the floor.

DEXTER: That's right. That should do it. Now, don't forget, Lina. The mike is on your shoulder.

He pulls microphone from corsage on her shoulder, shows it to her, and puts it back.

And whatever you say goes through the wire onto the record. Now, please, Lina—talk into the mike.

LINA *(wearily)*: Yeah.

DEXTER: Oh, and don't make any quick, jerky movements or you might disconnect it. Okay, let's go. Quiet.

FIRST ASSISTANT: Quiet.

SECOND ASSISTANT: Quiet.

51

DEXTER *(beyond caring)*: Roll 'em.

He exits into sound booth. As the garden scene begins again, we see Simpson enter door from the outside, while Lina speaks.

LINA *(clearly heard at last)*: "Oh, Pierre, you shouldn't have come. You are flirting with danger."

As Simpson walks forward, he trips over a wire.

SIMPSON *(angrily)*: What's this wire doing here?

WORKMAN: Shhhhh!

SIMPSON: It's dangerous.

The workman tries to stop him, but Simpson gets there first, bends down, and yanks the wire. It is the wire connected to Lina's mike, and she is pulled backward, head over heels, from the bench, in all her eighteenth-century splendor. She screams wildly. Dexter, inside the recording booth, pulls his cap off and buries his face in it with a hysterical groan.

Theater Exterior

A rainy night. The theater marquee reads:

MAJOR STUDIO
PREVIEW
TONIGHT

A car pulls up. Kathy, Don, and Cosmo get out, all dressed for the weather in raincoats. They're obviously by now a close threesome.

Interior Theater, Lobby

COSMO: You two had better not go into the theater together.

DON: Yeah. Lina's probably waiting right inside the door. *(Taking her hand)* Oh, Kathy—how I wish—

KATHY: Don't worry, Don. I'll be leading the cheering section in the balcony. Good luck.

She exits toward the balcony stairs, and Cosmo and Don start toward the orchestra section.

Inside the Theater

A large audience is eagerly awaiting the studio preview, and there is a feeling of excited anticipation as the first titles flash on the theater screen:

DON LOCKWOOD

and

LINA LAMONT

in

THE DUELING
CAVALIER

100% ALL TALKIE

Sitting in the back row are Dexter and Simpson—with Simpson looking calm, and Dexter chewing his nails. Lina is wearing dark glasses, which she removes as the film begins. She looks excited and pleased. Don is seated next to her with Cosmo. He gives Cosmo a "well, here goes nothing" look and smiles.

On Theater Screen

A handsome setting in the French palace. Down the grand hall comes Lina as Yvonne, a French noblewoman, looking beautifully regal, flanked by her ladies-in-waiting. She is pensively toying with a string of pearls around her neck. There is a terrific noise coming from the screen.

Last Row of Theater

SIMPSON *(as the noise continues)*: What's that—the thunderstorm outside?

DEXTER *(unhappliy)*: It's those pearls, Mr. Simpson.

On Theater Screen

LINA *(she is mouthing her words carefully, but the same old Lamont voice emerges from this regal figure, plus terribly recorded sound)*:

"I am the noblest lady of the court. Second only to the Queen. Yet I am the saddest of mortals in France."

LADY-IN-WAITING *(in a beautifully modulated voice)*: "Why, what is the matter, milady?"

LINA: "I'm so downhearted, Theresa. My father has me betrothed to Baron de Landsfield, and I cahn't stan' him."

The "cahn't" comes out very British, but the "stand" is still very flat and nasal.

LADY-IN-WAITING: But he is such a catch. All the ladies of the court wish they were in your pretty shoes.

LINA *(sadly)*: My heart belongs to another—Pierre de Battaille. *(She pronounces it Bat-al-lee)* Ever since I met him, I cahn't git him out of my mind.

Last Row of Theater

LINA *(turning to Don proudly)*: Good and loud, huh?

On Theater Screen

The garden scene, with Lina sitting on bench, looking sad. Don enters, looking very fraught. He sees his love, and comes forward to her, throwing away his staff as he does so. The staff hits the ground, making a sound like a bomb detonating. He archly puts his hands over her eyes, she reacts happily, and as he takes his hands down, she speaks.

LINA *(still moving her head from side to side, with her voice fading and getting loud by turns)*: "OH, PIERRE, YOU shouldn't have COME. YOU'RE flirting with danGER. THEY WILL surely find you OUT. YOUR head is much TOO VALUABLE."

Last Row of Theater

DEXTER *(as Simpson eyes him balefully)*: She never could remember where the microphone was, boss.

On Theater Screen

Don's acting, on his entrance to Lina's side, has been bounding and florid in the silent-movie tradition, and now, as he speaks his first lines, he is grandiose, and what with the awful, strained quality of sound, he is coming across ludicrously.

DON *(kneeling by her side)*: " 'Tis Cupid himself that called me here, and I, smitten by his arrow, must come charging to your side, despite the threats of Madame LaGuillotine."

LINA: "But the night is full of our inemies."

She taps him on the shoulder with her fan. It makes a large noise.

In the Audience

The theater audience is laughing raucously.

BOY *(loudly)*: Hey, Lina, what'cha hittin' him with—a blackjack?

On Theater Screen

DON *(kissing her hand)*: "Imperious princess of the night, I love you."

LINA: "Oh, Pierre."

DON *(kissing her again and again on the arm, the shoulder, in a transport of passion)*: "I love you—I love you—I love you—I love you—I love you—I love you—I love you—I love you—I love you—I love you."

The "I love yous" grow more intense and silly with each succeeding one, and the growing shrieks of laughter from the theater audience almost drown them out.

In Theater Audience

A MAN: Did somebody get paid for writing that dialogue?

Theater Lobby

A man is standing there and hears the roars of laughter coming from inside. He turns to a ticket-taker by the door.

MAN: Sounds like a comedy inside.

TICKET-TAKER: It's a Lockwood-Lamont talkie.

MAN: What?

WOMAN *(leaving theater)*: This is terrible.

On Theater Screen

Don and a manservant are in the midst of a scene. The servant is brushing Don's pantaloons when the picture on the screen suddenly jumps out of frame. There is a terrible noise on the soundtrack as the picture freezes, off-kilter, then jumps back into position again, and resumes running. Don takes some snuff from a box held out to him by his servant, who exits— but there is something very wrong with the sound and the image.

Back Row of Theater

SIMPSON *(puzzled)*: What's that?

DEXTER *(miserably)*: The sound. It's out of synchronization.

SIMPSON: Well, tell them to fix it!

DEXTER *(dashing out)*: Yes, sir.

On Theater Screen

DON *(reading a message and then speaking, his mouthing and actions a few beats behind the sound)*: "Yvonne! Captured by Rouge Noir of the Purple Terror? Oh—oh, my sword! I must fly to her side. Yvonne, Yvonne—my own!"

After the soundtrack of this scene is finished, we see Don mouthing "Yvonne—my own!" in silence, before he exits. The scene on screen shifts to Lina on a balcony, struggling in the villain's clutches. The sound is still out of synch, so that when the villain speaks, Lina's voice seems to issue from his mouth, and so forth, through the scene.

VILLAIN *(with Lina's voice)*: "Pierre!"

LINA *(Villain's voice)*: "Pierre is miles away, my witch."

VILLAIN *(Lina's voice)*: "No, no, no!"

LINA *(Villain's voice)*: "Yes, yes, yes!"

VILLAIN *(Lina's voice)*: "No, no, no!"

LINA *(Villain's voice)*: "Yes, yes, yes!"

VILLAIN *(Lina's voice)*: "No——nooo——nooooooo."

Lina's voice slides into a bass and then grinds to a stop, as the film, with the image of the villain talking, slows down and finally stops on a held frame.

Theater Lobby

Lina, Simpson, Don, Dexter, and Cosmo are huddled together on the side, miserable, except for Lina, who looks quite pleased with herself, while the people come pouring out of the theater.

WOMAN: This is a scream.

MAN: Give me pictures like *The Jazz Singer*.

BOY *(imitating Don)*: I love you, I love you, I love you, I love you, I love you, I love you!

SIMPSON *(dejected)*: We're ruined. We're all ruined.

DON *(very low)*: You can't release this picture.

SIMPSON: We've got to. We're booked to open in six weeks all over the country. *(Looking around for reassurance, with a forced smile)* But you, you're such big stars, we might get by.

WOMAN *(leaving)*: I never want to see that Lockwood and Lamont again.

ANOTHER WOMAN: Wasn't it awful?

MAN: This is the worst picture ever made.

LINA *(brightly)*: *I* liked it!

Don's House

A Spanish-mission-style mansion. Through an open window, Don, Kathy, and Cosmo can be seen at a dining-room table, with half-empty plates in front of them and some glasses of milk. Then, as Don speaks, we are inside the room.

DON *(totally defeated)*: Well, take a last look at it. It'll be up for auction in the morning.

COSMO *(overbright)*: Ah, you're out of your mind. Besides, it's Saturday. No bank's going to foreclose until Monday.

KATHY *(unconvincingly)*: It wasn't so bad.

COSMO: Well, that's what I've been trying to tell him.

DON: No. There's no use kidding myself. Once they release *The Dueling Cavalier*, Lockwood and Lamont are through. The picture's a museum piece. I'm a museum piece.

KATHY: Well, things went wrong with the sound. If you'd just get the technical end straightened out—

DON: No, it wasn't that. Look, this is sweet of both of you, but I—Something happened to me tonight. I . . . I . . . Well, everything you ever said about me is true, Kathy. I'm no actor. I never was. Just a lot of dumb show. I know that now.

COSMO: Well, at least you're taking it lying down.

The three have each picked up their own plates and glasses and are headed for the kitchen.

They enter the kitchen and start putting dishes on the table.

DON: No. No kidding, Cosmo. Did you ever see anything as idiotic as me on that screen tonight?

COSMO: Yeah. How about Lina?

DON: All right. I ran her a close second. Maybe it was a photo finish. Anyway, I'm through, fellas.

KATHY: Don, you're not through.

COSMO: Why, of course not. Why, with your looks and your figure, you could drive an ice wagon or shine shoes.

KATHY: Block hats—

COSMO: Sell pencils.

KATHY: Dig ditches.

COSMO: Or worse still—go back into vaudeville.

Cosmo sings a few lines of "Fit as a Fiddle."

DON *(depressed)*: Too bad I didn't do that in *Dueling Cavalier.* They might've liked it.

KATHY *(suddenly lighting up)*: Why don't you?

DON: What?

KATHY: Make a musical.

DON: A musical?

COSMO: Sure. Make a musical. The new Don Lockwood. He yodels, he jumps about to music.

DON: Oh. The only trouble is that after they release *Dueling Cavalier* nobody'd come to see me jump off the Woolworth Building into a damp rag.

COSMO: Well, why don't you turn *The Dueling Cavalier* into a musical?

DON: *The Dueling Cavalier?*

COSMO *(looking at a calendar on the wall)*: Sure. We've got six weeks before it's released.

KATHY: Yeah. Add some songs and dances, trim the bad scenes, add a couple of new ones—

COSMO: And you got it.

DON: Hey! Hey, I think it'll work.

KATHY: Of course.

COSMO: It's a cinch.

DON: You know, it may be crazy, but we're going to do it. *The Dueling Cavalier* is now a musical.

COSMO: Hot dog!

KATHY: Hallelujah!

DON *(showing the date on the calendar)*: Whoopee! Fellas, I feel this is my lucky day. March twenty-third.

COSMO: Aw, no, your lucky day is the twenty-fourth.

DON: What do you mean the twenty-fourth?

COSMO: It's one-thirty already. It's morning.

KATHY: Yes. And what a lovely morning!

She looks out the window, and we see that it is pouring.

Kathy, Don, and Cosmo sing and dance "Good Mornin'." (See film stills 26, 27.) Elated, the three of them sing and dance all over the kitchen and then into the living room, where, finding a rack with hats and coats on it, they improvise costumes of many lands—Scotch, Spanish, French cancan, etc.— dancing in the various styles suggested, until they collapse, happy and exhausted, on the couch.

DON *(his elation fading)*: Hey! Hey, we can't make this a musical.

COSMO: What do you mean?

DON: Lina.

COSMO AND KATHY *(depressed)*: Lina.

COSMO: She can't act. She can't sing, and she can't dance. A triple threat.

DON: Yeah.

Kathy suddenly starts laughing.

COSMO: What's so funny?

KATHY: I'm sorry. I was just thinking. I think I liked her best when the sound went off and she said "yes, yes, yes." *(She imitates the deep voice of the villain)*

COSMO *(in Lina's high voice)*: "No, no, no."

KATHY *(again in the low voice)*: "Yes, yes, yes."

COSMO: "No, no . . ." Wait a minute. Wait a minute. I am just about to be brilliant. Come here, Kathy. Come here. Now, sing.

KATHY: Huh?

COSMO: I said, sing. *(Sings)* "Good mornin'."

COSMO AND KATHY *(sing)*: "Good mornin' . . ."

COSMO *(over and above singing)*: Now, Don, keep your eyes riveted on my face—watch my mouth.

As Kathy sings, Cosmo mouths the words in perfect synchronization with her singing—and it looks as though the sound were coming from him.

COSMO: Well, convincing?

DON: Enchanting. Why?

COSMO: Don't you get it? Use Kathy's voice. Lina just moves her mouth, and Kathy's voice comes over singing and talking for her.

KATHY: That's wonderful.

DON: No—no. I couldn't let you do it, Kathy.

KATHY: Why not?

DON: Because you wouldn't be seen. You'd be throwing away your own career.

KATHY: It has nothing to do with my career. It's only for this one picture. The important thing now is to save *The Dueling Cavalier*, save Lockwood and Lamont.

COSMO: Yeah.

DON: Well—well, all right, if it's only for this one picture. But— do you think it'll get by?

KATHY: Of course it will.

COSMO: Sure. And it's simple to work the numbers. All you gotta do is dance around Lina, and teach her how to bow.

DON: All right, we'll go to R. F. and spring it on him in the morning.

KATHY *(kissing him)*: Don, you're a genius. *(See film still 28.)*

COSMO: I'm glad you thought of it.

KATHY: Oh, Cosmo.

She kisses him, and he falls over backwards.

Street Outside Kathy's House

Don and Kathy are kissing in the doorway. It is raining hard. A cab is waiting in the street.

DON: Good night, Kathy. See you tomorrow.

KATHY: Good night, Don. Take care of that throat. You're a big singing star now—remember? This California dew is a little heavier than usual tonight.

DON: Really? From where I stand, the sun is shining all over the place.

They kiss again, Don holding his umbrella over them. As Kathy goes in, Don looks up at the rain, motions the cab to drive off, closes his umbrella, starts strolling and singing the introduction to "Singin' in the Rain."

In the pouring rain, Don, happy and in love, sings and dances in the wet street, jumping up on the lamp post, sloshing joyously through puddles, letting the water from a rain pipe hit him in the face, balancing like a tightrope walker on the curb, and finally, in an outburst of exuberance, kicking up water in the gutter like a kid. He notices a policeman eyeing him with suspicion, collects himself, and after getting up on the sidewalk, strolls off, drenched and in love with life. (See film stills 29, 30, 31.)

Simpson's Office

Simpson is behind the desk, Cosmo and Don in front of the desk.

SIMPSON: Why, that's wonderful—that's wonderful! *(Getting up)* Now, look, we'll keep the whole thing secret until we're ready to release, just in case it doesn't come off. But I'm a little worried about Lina. She doesn't like Miss Selden. There might be fireworks.

DON: I guarantee you, Lina won't even know she's on the lot!

SIMPSON *(convinced and excited)*: Okay, boys! This is great! *The Dueling Cavalier* can be saved! *(He jumps to his feet and starts pacing back and forth, thinking excitedly)* Let's see—*Dueling Cavalier* with music—the title. The title's not right. We need a musical title. Cosmo?

COSMO *(jumping to his feet and starting to pace also)*: How about *The Dueling Mammy*—uh, no, no— *(silence while they pace)* I've got it! *(They all stop pacing and stare at him)* Uh, no, no, no, no—

They resume pacing. Cosmo claps his hands jubilantly, stopping everyone again. Triumphantly:

The Dancing Cavalier!

SIMPSON *(jubilant)*: *The Dancing Cavalier*! That's it! That's great! Cosmo, remind me to make you a scriptwriter.

COSMO *(offhandedly, offering a box of cigars)*: Thanks, R. F., have a cigar.

They resume pacing in opposite directions, chewing on cigars.

SIMPSON: Thanks. But what about the story—we want to have modern musical numbers. Cosmo?

COSMO *(thinking quickly with a feeling that he can do no wrong at this point)*: Let's see—how this? We throw a modern section into the picture. The hero is a modern young hoofer in a Broadway show. Right?

SIMPSON: Right.

COSMO: He sings, dances—right?

SIMPSON: Right.

COSMO: Well, one night backstage, he's reading *The Tale of Two Cities* between numbers, see? A sandbag falls on his head, and he dreams he's back during the French Revolution! This way we get in modern dancing numbers—Charleston-Charleston—but in the dream part we can use all the costume stuff—right?

SIMPSON *(more excited)*: Sensational! Cosmo, remind me to give you a raise.

COSMO: Oh, R. F.—

SIMPSON: Yes.

COSMO: Give me a raise.

Recording Stage

Kathy is at the microphone singing "Would You?" There is a full orchestra present, with Cosmo conducting and Don watching her. Don is standing beside her, and her singing is directed at him. In the course of one chorus of the song, we see the whole recording synchronization process, and finally how it looks on the screen. As the chorus of the song continues, we see the playback machine and hear Kathy's voice singing "Would You?" Lina is mouthing the words as Don and Cosmo look on. Lina is having trouble with the synchronization. On the sound stage, Dexter holds up the slate. Lina is in the eighteenth-century garden set continuing the song to Kathy's voice. In the projection room, Lina is in the same eighteenth-century garden set continuing the song, and we see it as a scene from the picture in black and white projected on the screen in the projection room. Simpson, Don, and Cosmo watch until the end of the number. The screen darkens, the lights go up.

SIMPSON *(happily)*: It's perfect! That Selden girl is great! When the picture is released, I'm going to give her a big build-up! Don, how much is there left to do?

DON: One more scene—and a number left to shoot.

SIMPSON: What number?

DON: It's a new one—for the modern part of the picture. It's called "Broadway Melody." It's the story of the young hoofer who comes to New York. First, we set the stage with a song. It goes like this.

This is a big production number shown as it will appear in The Dancing Cavalier. *In a setting of Broadway neon signs, Don sings "Broadway Melody," followed by a many-sectioned number, using mainly the two songs "Broadway Melody" and "Broadway Rhythm" to tell the story of the young hoofer, played by Don, whom we first see arriving in the big city with his little suitcase, having a hard time, then getting a chance to audition at a club. There, a big gangster and his henchman arrive, with a devastating girl who flirts with him, dances passionately with him, but drops him for the gangster's offer of a diamond bracelet. Determined to make good, the hoofer rises in show business until he is a big star, and in an elaborate gambling casino, he meets the girl again, and visualizes himself dancing a love duet with her in an imagined paradise. Back to reality, he approaches her, but she disdains*

64

his advances again, turning away and flipping a coin, the way her gangster lover does. Don, cynically amused, sees a new fresh kid arriving with his little suitcase, just as Don had done, to conquer Broadway. Back in the setting of neon signs, Don sings the end of "Broadway Melody." (See film stills 32 through 43.)

DON: Well, that's the idea of the number, R. F. What do you think of it?

SIMPSON: I can't quite visualize it. I'll have to see it on film, first.

COSMO: On film, it'll be better yet.

SIMPSON: Now, get going, fellows. Don't forget. You've got to have that Selden girl re-record all of Lina's dialogue.

COSMO: It's all set up.

SIMPSON: And remember, don't let Lina know about it.

Inside the Looping Room

This is a room where errors in dialogue can be corrected. The actors watch and listen to a line on the screen, and then, matching the timing, can record a new reading. Don and Kathy are standing in front of a microphone with earphones on and watching the screen, which is placed high on one wall. The room is quite dark. Across from the screen is the booth where the technician sits, making the recording and checking the readings. Near the screen, a red light flashes.

COSMO: All set in there?

TECHNICIAN *(in booth)*: Right.

LINA'S VOICE *(from screen)*: "Nothing can keep us apart. Our love will last till the stars turn cold."

COSMO: All right, Kathy—go ahead.

As Lina's image comes on the screen, Kathy says the line.

KATHY: "Nothing can keep us apart. Our love will last till the stars turn cold."

COSMO'S VOICE: That's great! Perfect! Cut!

The lights come up and Don looks at Kathy.

DON: Till the stars turn cold . . . *(He kisses her softly)* I love you, Kathy.

KATHY: Don, I—

DON: Kathy, I can't wait till this picture is finished. Then, no more secrecy. I'm going to let Lina know—let everyone know.

KATHY *(happily)*: Your fans will be bitterly disappointed.

DON *(lovingly)*: From now on there's only one fan I'm worrying about. *(See film still 44.)*

As they kiss, the door is flung open and in come Lina and Zelda.

ZELDA *(pointing to Don and Kathy)*: There!

LINA *(registering the scene)*: Oh!

ZELDA: What did I tell you, Lina!

LINA *(beside herself)*: Oh, Don! Zelda—thanks, you're a real pal! *(Furious)* I want that girl off the lot at once! She's not going to be *my* voice! Zelda told me everything!

DON: Thanks, Zelda—you're a real pal.

ZELDA *(sweetly, exiting)*: Any time, Don.

KATHY: Now look, Miss Lamont—Don and I happen—

LINA *(hurt and angry)*: Don! Don't you call him "Don"! I was calling him "Don" before you were born! I mean— Oh! You were kissing him!

DON *(getting worked up)*: *I* was kissing *her*! I happen to be in love with her.

LINA: That's ridiculous! Everyone knows you're in love with me!

DON: Now, Lina, try and understand this—I'm going to marry her.

LINA: Silly boy—she ain't the marrying kind. She's just a flirt, trying to get ahead by using you. Well, I'll put a stop to that— I'm going to see R. F. right now!

COSMO: You're a little too late, Lina—the picture's all finished; and if this girl weren't in the picture, *you'd* be finished, too!

LINA: As far as I can see, she's the only one who's finished! Who'll ever hear of her!

DON: Everybody! Why do you think Zelda's in a sweat? Because Kathy nearly stole the picture from her.

COSMO: Sure, she's just doing you a favor helping you on *Dancing Cavalier*.

DON: And she's getting full screen credit for doing it!

LINA *(exploding)*:You mean it's gonna say on the screen that I don't sing and talk myself!

DON: Of course—what did you think!

LINA *(the realization sinking in)*: But they can't do that!

COSMO: It's already done.

DON: And—there's a whole publicity campaign being planned!

LINA *(outraged)*: Publicity! They can't make a fool out of Lina Lamont! They can't make a laughingstock out of Lina Lamont! What do they think I am—dumb or something! Why—I make more money than—than —Calvin Coolidge—put to*git*her! *(She stamps out)*

Newspaper Page
Picture of Lina: "Glamorous Lina Lamont."
Headline reads: DORA BAILEY'S DAILY INTERVIEW: LINA GREATEST SINGING AND DANCING STAR, SIMPSON SAYS.

Simpson's Office
Simpson and publicity men. Rod is reading from a paper. Simpson looks stunned and angry.

ROD *(reading)*: "Monumental Pictures wildly enthusiastic over Lina's singing pipes and dancing stems."

SIMPSON: I never said that!

ROD *(reading)*: "Premiere tomorrow night to reveal Lina Lamont big musical talent." Boss, you can't pull a switch like this on the publicity department!

OTHER PUBLICITY MAN: We were all prepared for the campaign on Kathy Selden, and then you do this! At least keep us informed . . .

SIMPSON: Now, wait a second, fellas—I don't know anything about this! I had nothing to do with it!

ROD: Well, what are we going to do?

Lina flounces in carrying the papers, with her picture and the articles in them.

LINA *(answering him happily)*: Nothing! You wouldn't want to call the papers and say Lina Lamont is a big fat liar!

SIMPSON: Lina! Did you send that stuff out!

LINA *(very pleased with herself)*: I gave an exclusive story to every paper in town.

SIMPSON: Lina, you'll never get away with this. Rod. Call the papers back.

LINA: I wouldn't do that if I were you, R. F.

SIMPSON: Don't tell me what to do, Lina!

LINA: What do you think I am—dumb or somethin'? I had my lawyers go over my contract!

SIMPSON *(nervously)*: Contract!

LINA: Yeah—and *I* control my publicity—not you!

SIMPSON *(angrily)*: Yah?

LINA: Yah—the studio's responsible for every word printed about me; if I don't like it, I can *sue*! *(pronounced "syoo")*

SIMPSON *(shaken)*: What?

LINA: I can syoo! If you tell the papers about Kathy Selden, it would be *(Very grandly, like an elocution student)* "deteremental and deleterious to my career." I could syoo you for the whole studio! *(Hands him contract open to a certain page)*

SIMPSON *(on the defensive)*: That's a lot of nonsense.

LINA *(triumphantly)*: Says so—right here! *(Shows him; he reads to himself)* "Contract dated June 8, 1925—paragraph thirty-four—subdivision letter A—the party of the first part—" That's *me*!

He looks up at her.

SIMPSON *(beaten)*: You win, Lina.

ROD: We better take Kathy Selden's credit card off the screen.

SIMPSON *(furious, and angry with himself)*: All right—all right. Let's just get this premiere over with!

> *The publicity men exit. He turns to Lina, displeased and helpless.*

Satisfied?

LINA *(brightly)*: Only one little thing more.

SIMPSON *(sarcastically)*: Yes? Want me to change the name of the studio to Lamont Pictures Incorporated?

LINA *(very big-eyed)*: Oh, R. F., you're cute. No, I was just thinking—you've given this girl a part in Zelda's picture and you're going to give her an even bigger one in the next?

SIMPSON: So what?

LINA *(innocently)*: So! If she's done such a grand job doubling for my voice, don't you think she'd better go on doing just that—and nothing else?

SIMPSON: Lina, you're out of your mind!

LINA *(with an edge)*: After all, I'm still more important to the studio than she is!

SIMPSON *(angry and uneasy)*: Lina, I wouldn't do that to her in a million years. Why, you'd be taking that girl's career away. People don't do things like that!

LINA *(pulling herself to full height)*: People! *I'm* not people! I'm a *(She searches in the paper she is holding for the quote she wants and reads it triumphantly)* "shimmering, glowing star in the cinema firma*mint*!" It says so—*right here*!

Grauman's Chinese Theater

> *Crowds of people, spotlights, traffic moving slowly. The signs read:* PREMIERE TONIGHT—ALL SINGING—ALL TALKING—ALL DANCING. DON LOCKWOOD AND LINA LAMONT IN "THE DANCING CAVALIER."

Inside Grauman's Chinese Theater

The audience watching. Don and Lina are on the movie screen, in the last scene of the picture. Don is lying on the ground; Lina leans over him.

LINA: "Oh, Pierre, Pierre, my darling! At last I've found you! Pierre, you're hurt. Oh, speak to me—speak to me."

He raises his head and sings two lines of "Would You?" She joins him, singing the next two lines.

LINA *(speaking)*: "Oh, Pierre, hold me in your arms always."

We see Kathy, Cosmo, and others in the audience.

MAN *(in the audience)*: Lockwood's a sensation.

WOMAN: Yes, but Lamont. What a voice! Isn't she marvelous?

KATHY: It's going over wonderfully, isn't it?

COSMO: Yeah.

DON *(on screen)*: "Our love will last till the stars turn cold."

He starts singing, Lina joins him, and they end in harmony, in typical florid operetta style. They kiss and embrace. We see a statue of Cupid, and superimposed on it, the words "The End." Curtains close over the screen, as the audience applauds.

From the wings we see Don and Lina on stage—and hear the audience applauding wildly. Kathy and Cosmo join Simpson and Rod, as Don and Lina come off stage.

In the wings

SIMPSON: Congratulations, kids. We owe you a lot!

KATHY: Thank you.

DON *(embracing her)*: Kathy, we made it.

KATHY: Don, it's a miracle.

COSMO: It's great, Don. Just great. Oh, Lina, you were fabulous. You sang as well as Kathy Selden.

LINA: Yeah. And I'm gonna for a long time.

DON: Hey, what do you mean by that?

LINA: I mean she's gonna go right on singing for me.

DON: Listen, Lina, I thought something was cooking beneath those bleached curls of yours. Now, get this: Kathy's got a career of her own. She only did this for the one picture.

LINA: That's what you think.

ROD *(urging them on stage)*: Come on—come on!

Don and Lina run back on for a bow, then come off again.

COSMO: Lina's getting a little carried away, isn't she, boss?

SIMPSON: Yes. Yes, she is.

DON: Listen, you boa constrictor—don't get any fancy ideas about the future. Tell her, R. F. *(See film still 45.)*

LINA: Never mind, R. F. Listen to that applause out there. And wait till the money starts rolling in. You're not gonna give all that up just because some little nobody don't want to be my voice!

ROD: She's got something there, boss. It's a gold mine.

KATHY: Part of that choice is mine—Miss Lamont. And I just won't do it.

LINA: You got a five-year contract, honey. You'll do what R. F. says.

DON *(angrily)*: Well, what'sa matter, R. F.? Why don't you tell her off?

SIMPSON: I . . . I don't know. I . . . I'm confused. This thing is so big, I—

ROD: Come on. They're tearing the house apart.

LINA: Oh!

SIMPSON: Go on. Take a curtain call.

Don and Lina take another bow.

COSMO: Simpson, I once gave you a cigar. Can I have it back?

SIMPSON: Oh, now, wait a minute, Cosmo—

LINA *(coming back)*: Listen to them. I'm an avalanche! Oh, Selden, you're stuck!

DON *(furious)*: R. F., if this happens, you'll get yourself a new boy, because I won't stand for it.

LINA: Who needs you? They'd come to see me if I played opposite a monkey!

SIMPSON (*being pushed too far*): Just a minute, Lina. Don's a smash, too. I'm going to say a few words now. I'm still running the studio.

LINA: I'm not so sure! You're the big Mr. Producer—always running things. Running me. Well, from now on, as far as I'm concerned, I'm running things.

SIMPSON: Lina Lamont Pictures, Incorporated, huh?

LINA: Yeah.

> *Off stage there are yells of "Speech! Speech!"*

SIMPSON: Lina, I think you've gone a little too far.

ROD: The speech, Don. They're yelling for a speech.

LINA: A speech? Yeah, everybody's always makin' speeches for me. Well, tonight I'm gonna do my own talkin'. *I'm* gonna make the speech.

ROD: No, please, Lina—

DON (*after exchanging a look with Cosmo*): W-wait a minute, Rod. Wait a minute. This is Lina's big night. And she's entitled to do the talking. Right?

SIMPSON (*in on the thought*): Right.

COSMO: Right.

On stage

> *On stage, Lina speaking into microphone, slowly, with "great-lady" air.*

LINA: Ladies and gentlemen, I cahn't tell you—

> *The audience reacts to the strange sound of her flat nasal voice.*

—how thrilled we are at your reception for *The Dancing Cavalier*, our first musi*cale* picture togither. If we bring a little joy into your humdrum lives, it makes us feel as though our hard work ain't been in vain for nothin'.

> *During the speech we see people in the audience looking puzzled at the sound of Lina's voice.*

MAN IN AUDIENCE: Hey, she didn't sound that way in the picture.
Suddenly a voice rings out in the balcony.
VOICE: Hey, cut the talk, Lina! Sing!
All through the house the audience picks up the cry of "Sing! Sing!" As Lina hears the audience calling, she suddenly looks very frightened and horrified. She attempts to cover with a sickly smile as Don, looking very pleased, bows to her deferentially from the wings.
VOICES: Sing, Lina! Sing a song!
Lina looks trapped, hesitates, and then gestures to the audience, indicating, "Just a moment," and attempting to smile graciously, runs to the wings.

In the wings
DON *(with a glint in his eye)*: I've got an idea. Come on, now, listen—
Don, Simpson, and Cosmo go into a huddle as crowd voices off stage continue to shout, "Sing! Sing, Lina!"
LINA *(beside herself)*: What am I gonna do? What am I gonna do?
Simpson, Don, and Cosmo break huddle.
SIMPSON: Lina, we've got it. It's perfect. Rod, get a microphone set up back of that curtain. Kathy—come here.
ROD: Okay.
SIMPSON: Lina—Kathy will stand back of there and sing for you.
LINA: You mean she'll be back of the curtain singing, and I'll be out in front doing—like in the picture?
COSMO: That's right.
KATHY *(shocked)*: What?
DON: You gotta do it, Kathy. This thing is too big.
SIMPSON: Of course she's got to do it. She's got a five-year contract with me. Get over to that microphone, Selden.
DON *(icily)*: You heard him, Kathy. Now, do it.

KATHY: I'll do it, Don, I'll do it—but I never want to see you again on or off the screen.

COSMO: Now, come on, Lina.

On stage

Lina walks out on stage smiling and composed to the mike in front of the curtain as applause dies down. There is an orchestra in the pit.

ORCHESTRA LEADER: What are you going to sing, Miss Lamont?

Lina looks hesitant for a moment.

KATHY *(not seen by the audience, whispering toward the curtain)*: "Singin' in the Rain."

LINA: Er—"Singin' in the Rain."

ORCHESTRA LEADER: What key?

KATHY *(whispering)*: A flat.

LINA: A flat.

The orchestra goes into the song. From the front we see Lina apparently singing. The illusion is perfect. Behind the curtain we see Kathy singing.

In the wings we see Don, Cosmo, and Simpson watching. From this angle we can see Lina in front of the curtain, the side of the curtain itself, and Kathy in back of it, singing into the microphone. The three men move to stand around the ropes that pull the curtain. Lina is mouthing away, and making a flapping gesture with her elbows in time to the music. Near the end of the first chorus, the three men start flapping their elbows the same way, and then start pulling on the ropes, raising the curtain. On stage we see Lina continuing, and as the curtain rises, Kathy revealed behind her singing, now in full view of the audience. The crowd starts laughing, but Lina continues, oblivious to what is happening. Then Cosmo goes out on stage, and pushing Kathy aside gently, picks up the song in a roaring baritone. We see Lina for a second or two with this masculine voice seeming to come out of her throat, as the crowd collapses with laughter. Then, horrified, she stops and dashes off the stage. Kathy, truly bewildered, looks around, and suddenly runs down the steps from the stage to the audience, and begins rushing up the aisle to escape. Don runs out on the stage.

DON: Ladies and gentlemen, stop that girl!

There are ad libs from the audience.

That girl running up the aisle—stop her! That's the girl whose voice you heard and loved tonight. She's the real star of the picture. Kathy Selden!

The audience applauds. Kathy is stopped in the aisle, and turns toward Don. Don starts to sing "You Are My Lucky Star." There are tears in Kathy's eyes, as Don comes down the steps and reaches out to her. She sings part of the song, takes his hand, he leads her up on the stage. Cosmo has taken over conducting the orchestra in the pit. They sing together and embrace, and the scene dissolves into an outdoor sunlit scene: a huge billboard with Don's picture facing a picture of Kathy. The two of them are standing below and looking up at the billboard which reads:

SINGIN' IN THE RAIN
Don Lockwood   Kathy Selden
MONUMENTAL PICTURES

The song, sung by an off-stage chorus, reaches a soaring finish. It is the end.

(See film still 46.)